Y0-CBY-397

God bless you a
re ad —
In Jesus' love,
Leoda

# CONQUEST
# AND GLORY

## True Tales from the Land of the Taj

# CONQUEST AND GLORY

## True Tales from the Land of the Taj

Leoda Buckwalter

Evangel
Press
2000 Evangel Way
Nappanee, Indiana 46550-0189

*Conquest and Glory: True Tales from the Land of the Taj* © 1992 by Leoda Buckwalter. All rights reserved. No part of this book may be reproduced in any form or by any process or technique without written permission, except in case of brief quotations in critical articles or reviews. For information, write to Evangel Publishing House, P. O. Box 189, Nappanee, IN 46550.

Cover design: Weston Phipps

Library of Congress Catalog Card Number: 92-74955

ISBN: 0-916035-56-5

Printed in the United States of America

4 3 2 1

To my beloved sister,
Mrs. A. Abraham,
known to me as Chinnakutty,
who like her mother,
Aleyamma Oommen,
heralds forth the
coming dawn

# Contents

Preface

# Preface

When white, pure light hits an object and shatters into a thousand pieces, God produces a rainbow! Brilliant colors that merge earth tones with heavenly ones bend into an arc God specifically claimed as "my bow." Indeed, the Bible tells us he placed one around his throne in heaven. Have you ever wondered why?

Is he merely depicting the result of light smashing against obstacles, or perhaps showing the glory that results when heaven merges with earth?

Surely God expresses his infinite greatness. Nature shouts his delight in giving us the extra touch—every different snowflake, brilliant autumn leaves, breathtaking sunrises and sunsets, the amazing performance and resilience of the human body.

The psalmist spoke truthfully when he declared that the heavens declare God's glory and the earth shows his handiwork.

The Word tells us what happens when God infiltrates the darkness of sin and wickedness, smashing into a thousand or perhaps millions of pieces, but coming forth in the glorious beauty of Christ's redemptive work on Calvary. Who can estimate refracted Light in your heart and mine as darkness gives way to light, fear becomes trust, weakness turns to strength, and innate selfishness conforms to the image and likeness of Jesus?

Such transformation should be seen, the stories preserved. Therefore I bring to you *Conquest and Glory: True Tales from the Land of the Taj.*

These are a mere fraction of stories that could be gathered. They cover a time span from the turn of the twentieth century (Prosad series) to the late 1970s (the Sister Anne stories and others mentioning FEBA India).

Some relate to urban India, others to village life. Ethnic groups vary with Bengalis, Tamilians, Santals and Malayalees mentioned. We see the eternal Light penetrating the darkness of orthodox Hinduism, witchcraft, nominal Christianity, and the heart hungers found in a Muslim community.

I heard the stories from primary or secondary sources, experienced part, and read the reliable witness of others. To protect some of the main characters names and locations have been changed, but I personally knew Sister Anne, Elizabeth Liechti, and her friend Lilly Ammon. We visited Dipti Mission.

My purpose, then, is to preserve and celebrate Eternal Light penetrating and transforming darkness. May these accounts bring you closer to the One who deserves all praise and glory, our Lord Jesus Christ, the Lamb of God.

Leoda Buckwalter
Elizabethtown, Pennsylvania

To whom then will you liken God?
Or what likeness will you compare to Him?
The workman molds a graven image,
The goldsmith overspreads it with gold,
And the silversmith casts silver chains.
Whoever is too impoverished for such a contribution
Chooses a tree that will not rot;
He seeks for himself a skillful workman
To prepare a carved image that will not totter.

Have you not known?
Have you not heard?
Has it not been told you from the beginning?
Have you not understood from the foundations of the earth?
It is He who sits above the circle of the earth,
And its inhabitants are like grasshoppers,
Who stretches out the heavens like a curtain,
And spreads them out like a tent to dwell in.
He brings the princes to nothing;
He makes the judges of the earth useless. . . .

"To whom then will you liken Me,
Or to whom shall I be equal?" says the Holy One.
Lift up your eyes on high,
And see who has created these things,
Who brings out their host by number;
He calls them all by name,
By the greatness of His might
And the strength of His power;
Not one is missing. . . .

Have you not known?
Have you not heard?
The everlasting God, the LORD,
The Creator of the ends of the earth,
Neither faints nor is weary.
His understanding is unsearchable.

Isaiah 40:18-28
New King James Version

# The Battlefield

# Prosad and the specter

## Wielding the sword

"Kattromoni!" the girl gasped, writhing in labor pains. "Please . . . a boy!"

The clay idol on the corner shelf looked on, unmoved.

Kumdinni panted, "Pray for me, Mama Duoya. My strength's gone." The sweet-faced Bengali lady nodded. Her mother and sister also interceded as they hovered near the pallet in the corner. In that Himalayan cottage, set midst pine forests, the night wore on slowly . . . so slowly. Duoya made sure the lantern shone through the window at the right angle to aid her son, Prosad, sitting on the front verandah steps.

He looked at his watch, rose, and stretched. "Two o'clock," he commented. "I wonder what's happening." Entering the house the tall soldier crossed the living room and opened the bedroom door. His fourteen-year-old wife groaned in pain.

"Go, son," Duoya said softly. "When the baby comes, I'll call. I pray the gods favor you with a boy."

Prosad shrugged, then resumed his night vigil on the front verandah steps. A riot of flowers stretched in front of him. Their fragrance permeated the chill air and fireflies flickered in tantalizing flight patterns. Night sounds from the pine forests merged into the soothing music of the nearby stream and waterfall. A golden moon cast its glow on majestic snowcapped peaks.

"Oh, God . . . my God!" the man prayed. "I don't care whether it's a boy or girl. Just spare my wife and child."

A strange prayer from a member of an orthodox Hindu family!

Prosad claimed a long heritage of soldiering among his Bengali ancestors. He answered the insistent call of the frontier when the study of law in Calcutta's best universities paled. It was then, before the turn of the century, that Prosad applied for a permanent position as cashier, attached to the famous English Guide Regiment near Khyber Pass. The young soldier built his home in this mountain setting and brought his three dependents—mother, grandmother, and aunt—and later, his bride. Now the century was barely a year old when he awaited the birth of his first child.

The front door opened. His mother announced flatly, "It's a girl."

Disappointment covered her features, but the new father sprang up. "May I come?" he asked.

"No, Prosad, there's no hurry. Go to bed and sleep."

But sleep evaded him. The man paced the garden walks, alternating between joy and indignation—joy at the miracle of fathering a new life, anger at Hinduism and its low estimate of girls.

No bells, no feast, no celebration? It's just a girl! He spoke aloud, "Prosad, hear me! You'll let your daughter know she's loved. Moreover, you'll teach her to know the God who values even sparrows."

This wasn't his initial rebellion against the system. Indeed, while in college he studied the Bible as world literature, and during his reading of the Scriptures, he accepted Jesus Christ as his personal Lord. Yet he knew that open confession would forfeit his family position.

Prosad felt like a spy in an enemy camp. He maneuvered never to bow before Kali, the goddess of blood, nor to any other deity revered by his Hindu relatives. Sometimes he became discouraged. He often seemed to grapple with a ghost who threatened to make him recant and become a Hindu.

Was it the goddess Kali who dogged him? Against his will, on his mother's insistence, he permitted her to use one room in the house for worship. Kali's picture dominated everything in that sacred chamber. Blood dripped from her swords held by multiple arms. She stepped on the head of her aggressor while she leered in triumph, and extended her tongue in defiance.

Other lesser deities hovered around, stone idols that were worshiped by the devout Bengali widows. Kumdinni, his bride, brought her goddess with her, Kattromoni by name.

On one pretense or other Prosad kept aloof from the worship room. Now, as was his habit, he prayed under the open sky. Looking up he said, "My Lord Jesus, you've given me a daughter. Thank you, thank you! I'll name her Dipti—Light. I want her to reflect your radiance, even as the moon reflects the light of the sun. May she be more courageous than I. I promise to teach her to follow you."

He straightened, as though bracing for combat, and took a deep breath. He seemed to hear a mocking laugh, or was it just the wind whistling through the pines? No, there it was, stalking him. Good God! Was he losing his mind? Perhaps he was emotionally drained. He listened to hear the specter say, "You think you can snatch your daughter away from me? She's mine, not yours. She shall bow to me and worship me." The specter drew near and laughed again.

"Go! I command you in the name of Jesus!" Prosad commanded, pointing his forefinger defiantly. He then turned back to the verandah with a renewed sense of peace, and after spreading his mat where he would find shelter from the wind, he slept.

Upon entering their bedroom next morning, however, Prosad again sensed the presence of the enemy. The specter seemed to lift its head when the young father heard his young wife say, "Forgive me for not giving you a son. It's my fault. Please forgive me, and don't be angry."

She looked so frail and beautiful there in bed, the baby nestled beside her. Prosad caught her hand. "Kumdinni," he murmured, "my lovely one, our baby is precious. She'll be beautiful, like her mother. We'll name her Dipti, Light."

The girl nestled the baby closer and answered, "Not Dipti . . . no, no! I have promised my goddess, Kattromoni, to name her after her. She shall be Kattromoni."

"Oh?" Prosad drew a deep breath and straightened as the specter arose and moved near. Then he replied, "Let's compromise, Kumdinni. We'll call her Moni, Jewel. Even as a jewel catches the light to reflect it, she'll shine. You'd like that, wouldn't you?"

"Yes," she said with a smile. "I like that. She shall be Moni."

Prosad lifted the infant in his arms. As he cradled her he whispered, "Moni, my little one, I know whose jewel you'll be. Not Kattro's . . . no, not Kattro's!"

The specter receded, and Prosad tenderly kissed his infant daughter, then laid her beside her mother.

Moni became her father's joy and pride. From him she imbibed her love for nature. Climbing trees became a favorite sport, yet she often took time to sit by the waterfall, admiring nature's beauty. Father and daughter became almost inseparable, knowing a special bonding that held throughout all that would transpire. When Moni's mother developed a heart condition, Prosad sent her to Bengal to live, however he insisted that Grandma Duoya, who accompanied mother and child, bring Moni back. Kumdinni protested strongly, but the father's wish prevailed and the child returned to live in the pure air of the mountains. Indeed, throughout Moni's absence, Prosad had battled in prayer lest her little mind be turned to idol worship.

When she was four, father and daughter went on a trek. The rays of the setting sun shimmered on snowcapped peaks, turning them to gold, even as they began fusing into softer shades of rose and mauve. The young man caught his breath at the sheer splendor of the moment. His little girl stood quietly, hand in his, soaking in his excitement. She looked up and asked, "Did Goddess Kali make it, Daddy?" The wide sweep of her little arm took in both mountains and flowers.

A startled Prosad glanced down at his daughter. She looked up and asked a second time, "Did Goddess Kali make it?"

Anger surged within. Why should the specter of Hinduism follow him here? In the midst of God's marvelous creation, with his heart raised in praise to the True One, would his enemy dare snatch his most prized possession? In a protective sweep of his arm Prosad gathered the child to his breast and said, "No! No, Moni!"

She touched his face softly. "Not Kali, Daddy? Who, then?"

"The true God in the sky," he answered. "See how beautiful everything is? Not at all like Kali, is it?"

She nodded, and he continued, "God is like this—good, kind, and beautiful."

"Daddy, I want to see him."

"Sorry, darling, that's not possible."

"Why not? Isn't he real?"

"Yes, Moni, he's real." He walked with the child in his arms and sat on a rock. They watched the changing colors of the sunset on the snows while the wind blew softly through the trees. Prosad breathed a prayer. "Help me, Lord Jesus. I must make her believe."

"Feel the wind, Moni?"

"Yes, Daddy." She snuggled closer to her father.

"Can you see it?"

"I don't know. It makes me feel cold."

"And look at the leaves shaking on those trees. See the clouds moving across the sky? The wind is driving them. So we know something about the wind even though we can't see it."

He thought a moment, then said, "Moni, darling, you want to see God? You will know him by feeling his presence, by watching his wonders. See? He made the mountains, the sky, the trees, the flowers, everything! And, more than that . . . he made you and me. We must always love and serve him."

"Not Kali, Daddy? She didn't make it?"

"Not Kali, baby."

The specter, Prosad's enemy, seemed to leer, but from a distance, and Moni's father lifted his heart in praise.

She nestled in her father's arms and sighed, "I want to know God. Daddy, I think he must be like you."

The specter had left, and Prosad carried his daughter home with a light heart.

The next day Moni tiptoed into the worship room to look at the goddess, Kali, who stood on her husband's chest, a garland of human heads around her neck, each hand carrying a sword. Her long tongue stuck out in hatred and vengeance.

The child's horror slowly turned to anger. She felt she must answer this threat, so she stuck out her tongue. But the goddess didn't recant. The child tried again until her jaws ached. Furious that Kali had won in this contest, Moni determined to insult her. She pulled a stool from the corner, climbed on it, then placed her shoe on Kali's tongue! Satisfied that she had won at last, Moni climbed down and ran out to play.

Prosad's daughter relished this game of insult. Every morning Grandma Duoya worshiped, bringing fresh fruit and flowers. After she left, a little wisp of a child slipped into the half-darkened room, drew up a stool, climbed onto it and measured Kali's tongue with her foot.

But several days later the shoe left a telltale mark! A distraught Grandma Duoya surveyed the girl. "Come here, Moni!" she commanded, but Moni sped into the forest.

"I'll get her at bedtime. Meanwhile, I'd better see what amends I can make, lest the goddess wreak her vengeance."

The concerned woman hastened to the temple in the bazaar and paid a good sum of money to the local priest for saying a special *puja* to appease Kali. That evening Moni's grandmother took the tired child in her arms and soothed her. Then she said, "I want to talk to you."

"Grandma! What are you going to do with me?" Moni sat up, eyes filled with fear.

But the woman said kindly, "Nothing, dear. The goddess will avenge herself. You have angered her, Moni, and I don't know how to stop her. I gave the Brahman priest money today. Maybe the special *puja* he said will help. I just hope she won't kill you tonight."

Moni crept fearfully to bed. But, she reflected, she'd done this for days and nothing happened. Maybe the good God was watching over her. The weary child sighed, then fell asleep.

When Prosad came home that evening his mother began, "Son, that Moni. . . ."

"What, Mom? Where is she?"

"In bed. I sent her early. She's been very naughty today."

"What's the matter? Did she hurt herself or get sick?"

"No . . . but I can't guarantee what may happen tonight. . . . You see, Prosad, she's insulted the goddess, Kali."

He relaxed and said, "Tell me. . . . I'm all ears." With a hint of smile playing around his mouth the young man settled to hear his daughter's latest mischief.

"I noticed a mark on the goddess's tongue day before yesterday, Prosad. Baffled, I saw it again yesterday. Today I took a closer look, I definitely saw the imprint of the toe of a small shoe."

Lines of mirth began to creep around the corners of the man's eyes, but he listened quietly. His mother continued, "I suspected Moni, and this morning, Prosad, I caught her. Would you believe it? She slipped into the room, pulled the stool over in front of Kali, climbed on it and measured the tongue with her shoe!"

The distraught woman clasped her hands together, eyes cast upward. She missed the gleam of amusement in her son's eyes as she concluded, "That child has no respect for the Hindu religion, Prosad! What are you going to do about it?"

He laughed aloud. "Don't worry, Mom. This is just a childish prank. She'll be all right when she grows up."

"I'm not so sure," Duoya replied. "I don't ever see you worshiping the goddess, Prosad. How can you expect me to influence Moni over your negligence? She's completely loyal to you."

"Perhaps there's something to that," he admitted, "but if I were you, Mom, I wouldn't worry. Moni's just a child, and you can't take her actions too seriously. But keep me informed."

The next evening, however, Duoya warned her granddaughter by saying, "You've insulted Kali, Moni. She's the goddess of blood, and she'll kill you tonight."

Throughout the long night hours, the little four-year-old lay awake. Every corner shouted danger; every shadow seemed to move. But hour followed hour without the coming of the goddess. Finally, toward morning, the exhausted child fell asleep. She awakened to the singing of the birds and the bright sunshine streaming through her bedroom window.

Moni sat up, looked around, rubbed her eyes, then jumped out of bed. She pinched herself to see if she was real, then laughed a lilt of joy. The goddess hadn't killed her after all! She had won!

She tiptoed to the worship room. Grandma Duoya had come and gone. There lay the fresh, pungent marigolds on the altar. The child disdained the picture. It had lost its terror for her. Now her gaze rested on stone idols of varying heights in the room. She must conquer them too. She quickly placed them in a basket.

Where was Grandma? Working in the garden. The other two ladies kept to their side of the house until noon, and the cook had gone to market. So Moni pulled and pushed until she dragged the basket outside and dumped the idols into the nearest ditch. Then she ran to the camp where her father worked and met some of his friends. Before long the story of her escapade had passed from tent to tent. It finally reached Prosad. When he found her, he carried her home.

"I want to talk to you, Moni," he said before they entered the house. They sat beside the waterfall. Weary from her high adventure, after nearly a sleepless night, the child sobbed on her father's shoulder. He held her close and asked, "Moni, do you love Grandma?"

"Yes," she whimpered.

"Then why have you made her sad?"

"I don't want to hurt her, Daddy. I'm fighting Kali."

"Why?"

"Because Grandma said Kali would kill me last night . . . but she didn't! I'm not afraid of her anymore." Clasping him around the neck she whispered, "Daddy, I won."

Prosad couldn't suppress the laugh of triumph that welled up, but added, "You don't need to worry about Kali, darling. Your God and mine, the One who made heaven and earth, he's taking care of us. Look, Moni! Promise me you won't touch Grandma's idols again. She doesn't know what you and I know, but someday we'll tell her about the true God. Wouldn't that be much better?"

The little girl squirmed, then answered, "You know what, Daddy? Then she'll throw the idols away!"

"Will you tell Grandma you're sorry?"

With a nod and hug she said, "And . . . I won't ever . . . ever . . . do it again."

With a gentle kiss her father placed her on the ground, and taking her by the hand approached the house. He now knew she would be his secret weapon in their battle against Hinduism.

## Prosad's secret weapon

A proud father watched his daughter develop into a competent tomboy. Moni certainly didn't fit traditional patterns for an Indian girl, yet she exhibited a fine mind and body. Prosad considered any endeavor in her behalf worthwhile. She was, in fact, his secret weapon! Moni would do what Prosad had only begun . . . she would openly confess Jesus as Lord! And she would bless her own people in Jesus' name. He must prepare her for that hour.

He sat each evening with the tutor as they taught the girl several Indian languages. She also became an eager pupil of natural science and history. Father and daughter spent each weekend together. Consequently she became adept at horseback riding, mountaineering, and marksmanship. Her capabilities delighted her father's soldier friends.

But Grandma Duoya watched the girl mature with concern. When Moni turned eleven, she blossomed early and became an attractive young woman. "Now you must leave her in Bengal, Prosad," Duoya said. "She's too unprotected here."

"Mother, she has you and your sister," he remonstrated.

"True, son, but she's like a wild, beautiful deer! How can I control her? As for Nirmola, since mother's death, my sister is even more of a recluse than before."

Duoya had tried many times to instill fear of the goddess Kali into her grandchild, but without success. The girl stubbornly insisted on praying to the God who created the heavens and the earth. She told Duoya, "Grandma, no room can hold him. I must talk to him out under the sky."

The older woman thought this an excuse to get off the immediate compound. As a traditional Bengali widow, she confined her movements to the house and garden. Moni preferred the woods and waterfall. However, to help the girl gain some skills, Duoya offered to teach Moni cooking. The result pleased Prosad. He definitely approved of his daughter's culinary efforts.

Then came their annual month-long trek to Bengal. Moni dreaded going. Every year found her more and more distressed at her lack of freedom in her Bengal home. Mornings began with "Moni, don't do that! Indian girls don't act that way!" Evenings ended on the same sour note with her two brothers and sister, Usha, watching in wonder. Leela, the baby, was too young to understand.

Before this annual leave to Bengal, Kumdinni had written her husband, "Prosad, you must leave Moni with me this time. Bring all her things."

His solemn promise, made at the time of Moni's birth, rose before him. How far had the child progressed in her devotion to the true and living God? Would she, could she, reject Hinduism? Was she sufficiently strong to withstand family pressures? As long as he was near, her father could alleviate those demands, but once he returned to the mountains without Moni, then what?

Prosad prayed much, but the specter drew menacingly near, ready to snatch his firstborn, even as Hinduism had claimed all the rest. The man packed his bag with a heavy heart. He tucked his wife's last letter into a safe place. It read in part, "My brothers and I have made preliminary investigation of a fine young man from a wealthy family in good standing. He is the perfect husband for Moni. We'll finalize matters when you come, Prosad.

You can stay for the marriage, I hope? You will want to see her in her new home."

Moni married? She was yet a child!

From the moment her husband arrived with the girl and her grandmother, Kumdinni sought the appropriate time to bring up Moni's future. Somehow a week slipped by before her husband and she could discuss the question quietly in their room.

Kumdinni said urgently, "Prosad, you must leave Moni here. She's getting more and more out of hand."

"I hadn't noticed," he replied.

"No, of course you wouldn't. You spend your time with the men. She's in the women's courtyard."

He grunted, then said, "Confinement hampers any child, Kumdinni. Children need a degree of liberty to allow them to develop."

His wife faced him and raised her voice. "I thought you would understand! You're not advising girls' freedom, are you? It's not safe!"

"Why not? At least for Moni. She can protect herself, and she has a fine mind. What's all this talk about marriage? I'd rather see her well educated and blessing the world with her natural gifts."

"Nonsense!" Kumdinni retorted. "Every girl with a good reputation gets married and finds her joy in serving her family. Moni is willful and stubborn!"

Prosad's eyes flashed. "I object," he said. "Usha will be your kind. Calcutta's all she's ever known, but not Moni. She's different, and I feel we ought to give her the best education possible. If you insist on her remaining here, I'll pay all expenses for tutoring."

Their voices carried to the ears of the eleven-year-old who had come into the house for a drink of water. She pressed against the wall of their bedroom. She heard her mother's shrill voice, "You mean you would allow your child to compete in a man's world? Prosad! We'd lose caste!"

The soldier from the frontier answered, "Yes? Wouldn't that be better than hampering our daughter? Kumdinni, I simply don't see her fitting into a women's courtyard, pawn of a mother-in-law. Her entire training and nature is against such a life."

"That's my point! Had she stayed here, she would have been controllable. I simply don't have any alternative but marriage."

"But Kumdinni, she's yet a child."

"Prosad! Haven't you noticed your eldest becoming a young lady? She's marriageable now. Who knows what another year will do to her, especially in the freedom of the mountains, near that camp!"

The tall girl pressed closer to the wall. Marriage? How could she face that? She heard her father say, "Well, you can keep her home for several years. Give her loving attention and let her study. I'll leave her my money and pay for her higher education, perhaps in England. We'll let her develop on her own, choose her own faith, and bless the world with her natural talents."

"No, never! I'll never agree to higher education for Moni. She must become a disciplined girl. She must learn to live in a women's compound. Marriage is the only answer."

Prosad turned away sadly. The specter leered in triumph.

"It's totally your decision, Kumdinni. I wipe my hands of the matter."

"You'll stay for the wedding?"

"Never! I'll have no part in this!"

The specter receded, but the listening girl slipped out to the garden and wept.

The flurry of wedding preparations mollified Moni some, as did her grandmother's presence. Grandma Duoya promised to stay for several weeks following the marriage, a gesture that greatly comforted the girl.

In Prosad's absence, Kumdinni's elder brother, Lawyer Sen Bannerjee, officiated. The initial contract between the two families came first. Selected guests witnessed the legal engagement, held in the home of the bride. The Brahman priest chanted mantras and performed rites while members of Moni's household brought symbols of their authority over her—money, rice, *sarees*, and other items. Moni's uncle placed each on a pile as promise of renunciation. The groom received them one by one, thus lessening the ties of the girl with her own family. Then came the final cleavage when Ramesh Sircar tied a red string around her arm, to remain there until the wedding.

The marriage ceremony followed within several weeks, with the date set according to the horoscope. Kumdinni instructed her daughter, "Your husband's family is wealthy, and in many ways liberal. I'm sure you'll find them both interesting and cooperative. But you must try to win their love. Do exactly as they say, so they'll like you."

Her advice merely triggered new ideas of rebellion in Moni's active mind. Deep within she knew she would never remain in her husband's home. Since overhearing her parents' conversation, Moni determined to misbehave to the point of total rejection by her in-laws. Let the wedding take place!

So Moni complied gracefully, stunning her admirers in her brilliant red and gold *sarees*. Bejewelled and complimented on her wedding day, she felt happy and performed well. With downcast eyes, barely touching her food, she cast sidelong glances at the young man whom she met initially at their engagement. Now a married woman, Moni would go to the groom's house for ten days, then return to her parents until she was fourteen, at which time the final ceremony would be celebrated. Meanwhile, she would be known as Mrs. Sircar, and should her groom die she would be a widow.

Moni's plan for demolishing the marriage began the day after her arrival in the Sircar home. Suddenly she screamed at her mother-in-law! Her shrill voice startled the women into silence. "Keep quiet!" they demanded, but the more they reprimanded, the louder the girl yelled. Where was her shame?

The women drew back, but they still kept her.

Now for stage two!

Moni stole into the men's section and took a gun from the cupboard. Bringing it into the women's courtyard, she fired it into the air, fully expecting this to culminate the marriage. But the family decided to train her, and the men told the groom, "She's got nerve! Ramesh, you've found a jewel!"

Stage three!

The mango tree in the women's courtyard begged to be climbed. The harassed girl, constantly surrounded by demanding women, longed for privacy. On the seventh day she climbed the tree, and straddling a branch, watched the excited group below. That climaxed her feat! Her shocked spectators refused the bride any further place among them. Let the men say what they would! Moni returned home after seven days of married life.

She bounded into the house and threw her arms around her mother. "I've come," she announced triumphantly.

"Moni! You dreadful girl! You weren't due until Friday. What have you done?"

The girl looked at her unbelievingly. "Nothing, Ma! I haven't done anything wrong. I just fired their gun and climbed their tree. They'd better know what I'm like before they try to keep me."

"Aren't you even ashamed? You've disgraced your entire family!" Her mother buried her face in her hands and wept. "What can I do with this girl?" Her daughter turned and dejectedly walked away. Her triumph had suddenly become bitter. If only Daddy was here!

But Grandma Duoya met her and took her in her arms. "Come, Moni," she invited, "tell me about it." After hearing the story she murmured, "I understand, my girl, but I wonder what your father would say."

"He didn't want the marriage, Grandma," Moni insisted. "I heard him tell Mama. That's why he left before the wedding."

"I wondered," Duoya mused. "What is his wish? Do you know?"

"Oh, yes, he wants me to study and learn a lot so I can bless others."

"Moni," Grandma Duoya said, "you'll always be known as Mrs. Sircar. Look, dear," she pointed to the girl's hands still carrying the red paint of wedding decorations. She led her to the mirror and pointed to the red dot on her forehead and the red paint in the part of her hair. "These will wash out, but the fact that you are a married woman will never change."

"Oh, Grandma, take me back with you!"

"No, dear, you must stay here and learn the ways of the city. Your father is counting on you, and so am I. We know you have inner strength to face whatever comes. Promise me, Moni, you won't disgrace your family again."

The girl threw her arms around the woman. "Grandma Duoya, you've always loved me, even when I threw your idols away."

Duoya laughed, "And you've taught me a lot about the true God who made heaven and earth."

"Do you pray to him, Grandma?"

"Yes, Moni. I've left Kali worship."

"Oh, that's wonderful!" She kissed the woman and laughed. Duoya continued, "Moni, your father and I need you to represent us here. We're counting on you to uphold us, and we love you. We care! Will you promise?"

The girl thought quietly, then looked up, "Yes, Grandma, I promise. Tell Daddy I'm doing this for him."

In the Himalayas by the waterfall at the end of the long garden, Prosad sat on his favorite rock. His heart cried out, "Oh, God, what's the use? I'm tired of struggling. If only I had someone with whom I could talk and pray, it would help. None knows. Nobody understands!"

Night after night found him in his trysting place. Never, since Jesus Christ had changed his life during his college days, had Prosad touched such depths as now. He daily battled the temptation to join rowdy soldiers and drown his sorrow with drinking. His feet dragged past the club each evening, but resolutely, by sheer willpower, he turned toward the waterfall. There he renewed his pledge to the God of heaven and earth.

Then Big Joe Llewellyn, his Welsh friend, returned from his three-month vacation. From their first meeting Prosad sensed a change in him. Always cordial, Big Joe now exuded a new confidence, a quality of joy.

"You're different," Prosad commented. "What's happened to you?"

The soldier's eyes twinkled, and he chuckled. "So you've noticed?" he responded. "Come, let's walk. I'd like to tell you about it."

"The waterfall, Big Joe. That's where I meet the Lord."

The Welshman cast a quick glance at his Indian friend. "Which Lord, Prosad?" he asked.

"Jesus Christ . . . none other!"

"I didn't know where you stood on religion." Big Joe grinned, then said, "So you love him too? I didn't have any religion until I met my kind of man in Bombay. I figured such things are for sissies, but this chap—he has climbed mountains, hunted big game, yet he walks with God! You never saw a more saintly person . . . and he led me to Jesus Christ! I'll never be the same."

"Big Joe, you've just saved my life. I've hit bottom, and I need a Christian brother."

"What's the matter? Moni? Where is she? I haven't seen her."

"I've had to give her up, Big Joe." Prosad's voice choked, but he added, "She's in Bengal with her Hindu relatives. . . . I've fought all these years to give the girl a living faith in a living God. Now the family has married her into an orthodox Hindu home against my wishes. Big Joe. . ." his voice broke. "She's only eleven!"

"I hadn't heard," the Welshman said quietly.

"At birth I vowed I'd bring her up to love the true and living God."

"She will. You've taught her well, Prosad. Brother! You're my kind of man! You've also climbed mountains, bigger than I've ever seen. Now I know why you and Moni have meant so much to me. You'll win through, man, you will."

Prosad grasped the big hand thrust out toward him. In a hushed voice he answered, "Thank you, Big Joe. You came just in time. Thank you."

In Big Joe and Prosad's daily prayer sessions, Moni's name and needs became priority. It held her steady through tumult and trial. Her marriage aborted. She returned to an irate mother who bound her to the purdah system. She seldom left the courtyard since she was now a married woman!

Initially Kumdinni opposed Grandma Duoya's advice to let Moni study, but later employed two English ladies to tutor the girl. She little realized the great influence these missionaries would wield over Moni whose heart was completely open to the gospel. As a result, Moni became a stalwart Christian whose joyful witness caused profound changes in her home.

Kumdinni dismissed the tutors, then locked the girl in her room! But Moni managed to get a letter out to her father through a faithful servant who brought in food, and Prosad took a quick journey to Calcutta! He resolutely opened that door and decreed his daughter's complete freedom of choice.

The night he left she ran away, disguised as a boy, to the mission school. Her action resulted in her Uncle Sen, a prominent lawyer, charging the mission with kidnapping, but the Calcutta courts acquitted the school and missionaries.

Prosad continued to shield his daughter throughout her teen years and provided her with the finest education. He commended her on her public witness for Jesus Christ and always insisted that she live at home if she so desired. At baptism the girl took the name Prabhavati, servant of the Lord, but to her father she would forever remain his beautiful Moni, the jewel of Jesus. She became a respected and successful teacher and finally administrator in the same mission school that had given asylum when she fled from home.

Prosad then took early retirement to build a house near his daughter, facilitating daily visits at the end of her busy days.

His secret weapon had been tested and was now ready for action.

# The passing of the sword

The portly Bengali gentleman puffed slightly, due to the chill and the ten-minute walk from the bus stand to the bungalow tucked away up a long lane. He placed his briefcase under one arm and opened the gate with his free hand.

"Good morning, Sen," his brother-in-law called while hastening down the driveway. "I've been waiting for you."

They chatted casually, and the lawyer remarked to his retired relative from the army, "What color, Prosad! You have a way with flowers."

"I miss my garden in the Himalayas," the tall soldier admitted. "I've tried to reproduce a bit of it here since coming. Wish I could have transported the woods and waterfall. But you can't have everything, can you?"

"You're right, but do you like it here, so close to Calcutta? Quite different from life in the mountains. . . ."

"Like it here? Well, yes, especially since I can give Moni a home."

"Uh-huh, I thought so," the Bengali lawyer said with a smile. "How long were you in the mountains?"

"Twenty-five years, Sen. I was fortunate to have a permanent posting."

The men mounted the verandah steps, then turned to the corner room marked "office." Sen looked around with appreciation and said, "You have a beautiful home, Prosad. Did you design it?"

"Well, yes, with Moni's help."

"Is she interested in designing?"

"She has natural instinct in many things, so I take her advice when a woman's touch is needed. Kumdinni knows only the women's quarters, as you know, but, well—Moni is different." The tall man bowed slightly and said, "Excuse me, Sen. I'll order breakfast for us both."

His exit from the spacious office gave the lawyer a chance to examine his surroundings. "Army training," he murmured. "Like its owner, disciplined. Wonder what he wants."

Various family pictures and certificates hung on the walls. A tastefully arranged vase of flowers in the corner brightened the room. "Moni!" observed Sen. "That's her touch." He read a motto on Prosad's desk and drew back surprised, "Lo, I am with you always, even to the end of the world. Jesus Christ."

"Christ?" the Hindu lawyer puzzled. Was Moni's father interested in Christianity? Or, perhaps his daughter's charisma was drawing him toward her beliefs?

"Sorry to keep you waiting, Sen," Prosad apologized on his return. "Now everything's set for us to talk without interruption." He placed a cup of steaming tea in front of his guest, and the lawyer sipped it gratefully.

"Now to business," the retired soldier said as he took his seat behind the desk. "There's something I've kept from both Kumdinni and Moni, but I think you should know."

Sen, all attention, crossed one knee over the other, then asked, "What's that?"

"My army doctor tells me I have a bad heart condition."

"Oh, no!"

"Yes, and I think it time to put my business affairs in order. I want to know my family is cared for in the event of my sudden death."

"You speak openly about this. Aren't you afraid?"

"Not at all. Frankly, Sen, in my heart of hearts, I am a Christian. Ever since I attended St. Paul's College, I have followed Jesus Christ. Not even Kumdinni knows."

"But Moni does," her observant uncle remarked.

"Why do you think so?"

The lawyer chuckled. "You're as open as the day, Prosad! In fact, I begin to suspect you as the root cause for Moni's belief and actions."

Prosad laughed, then replied, "You're right, Sen! It's taken me awhile to face you with this. I thought you would be violently opposed, but I must come clean with my family even though all of you except Moni are Hindus. I want to be ready to meet my Lord Jesus when he calls."

The lawyer shifted uneasily. "I've been betting on Moni for years," he said slowly. "Kumdinni knows. What a clash we had when the girl took baptism!" He chuckled in retrospect. "Yes, my sister and I have had some tussles, and would you believe it? Though I outwardly headed up the opposition against the mission where Moni studied, I secretly cheered for her!"

"But I thought you're an orthodox Hindu!"

Sen chuckled again, then said, "I don't know what I am. Maybe you can help me." He added more seriously, "One thing I know. Both you and Moni have profoundly influenced my life. Every time I'm tempted to pull a shady deal, the thought of you two holds me steady. I want Moni to know she can always place confidence in her uncle Sen."

A knock on the office door interrupted their conversation. "May I come, Papa?" Benoy inquired.

"Yes, son," Prosad answered.

The young man brought in two trays, then said, "I'm off for college now."

"Fine . . . we'll take care of things. Thank you for bringing the food. Tell your mother I'll place the trays outside the door. We're not to be disturbed."

"Yes, Papa." The lad withdrew after greeting his uncle. Now the soldier turned to the lawyer and said with a short laugh, "Since I'm in my own house, do you mind my asking a Christian blessing?"

"What's that?"

"You've seen Moni bowing her head before she eats? We Christians thank God for supplying all our needs, and remember those less fortunate than ourselves. We call it saying grace."

"Sounds all right, man. Go ahead."

The meal concluded, the men turned to serious matters. Prosad opened the conversation again. "Sen," he said, "I want Moni to control the family after my death. Even though she's a girl, she's trained in administration. She's doing a good job in the mission school, and I trust her judgment. Do you agree, with the provision of your counsel?"

The lawyer said thoughtfully, "In our Bengali culture, this is irregular . . . but then . . . " and he smiled, "the entire circumstance is unusual. Yes, I agree to Moni, rather than Benoy, the eldest son."

"Thanks, Sen, and my body is never to be cremated. Moni should give me a Christian burial."

"Oh?" Sen raised his eyebrows in surprise. "Isn't that going a bit too far? Won't your mother object?"

"No, I don't think so," the soldier said quickly. His eyes twinkled as he added, "Moni's done an effective job on her grandmother. Grandma doesn't worship the goddess Kali now. In fact, she threw the pictures and idols away when we broke up housekeeping in the mountains."

"Yes, I see," the lawyer said with a chuckle. "Now, what about my sister?"

"That's another matter, Sen. Kumdinni's very attached to her goddess, but she does allow Moni freedom to read the Bible in the house. Frankly, I don't know how my wife will react to my having a Christian burial. She's the one I fear the most."

"I understand," Sen said, then asked, "But why not have a Hindu cremation?"

"I want to come clean. I've battled Hinduism all my life, ever since I believed in Jesus. I taught Moni to fear the true and living God. I educated her in good mission schools. I rejoice that she is blessing her generation. . . . I wish I could have blessed mine. She'll carry on my work, Sen. And I want her to know her father died confessing Christ openly. I must have a Christian burial."

Sen Bannerjee's mind whirled. What force compelled him to assent, "It shall be so, Prosad"?

"Yes," the soldier replied, "surely I have the right to leave this earth with a clean heart?"

The lawyer looked at his brother-in-law thoughtfully, remarking as he carefully matched his fingers, "Aren't you getting morbid, man? Why all this talk about death?"

"I'm suffering chest pains, and frankly, I'm troubled about a rumor that persists."

"What?"

"My bank is failing, and if it does, there go my life savings. . . ."

"Perhaps you should shift the money."

"Where to? These days all banks are uncertain, Sen."

The Bengali lawyer shrugged his shoulders. "Too true," he said. He looked up sharply and asked, "You have a will?"

"No, that's why I called you."

"Let's go over your business affairs, and I'll fix it for you."

An hour later Sen Bannerjee rose to leave. He grasped the soldier's hand and said earnestly, "My brother, I apologize for my part in the action against the mission. It was a game to me, one in which I never should have participated. Thank you for modeling a true man for me, Prosad."

Moni's father bowed his head, shoulders sagging. His mind reviewed the many times he maintained discreet silence in the face of opposition, yet shielded his child when she stepped out boldly.

Sen continued, "You've not only maintained your personal faith, you've always respected ours. And today you've exhibited a courage I highly admire." He looked up and placing his hand on Prosad's shoulder, concluded, "I hope you live a long time. The family needs you."

"Thank you, Sen," Prosad answered in a choked voice. "I don't think I have much time left. I want to be ready to meet my Lord."

With a deep breath, Sen concluded, "You will, and I'm proud of you."

Several weeks later, on a Sunday night, Prosad's daughter awoke suddenly from a bad dream. She seldom dreamed. Due to her active life as a physical education teacher, along with other school duties, she felt exhausted at the end of each day. Her quick walk home each evening and her quiet time with her family did much to relax Moni. Without exception, she returned to the mission compound to sleep soundly.

But today was different. Moni awakened before midnight, shaken by the dream. She had seen a coffin being carried from her father's room. "Who is it?" she cried, and heard the answer, "Your father."

"Impossible! He's in good health. It can't be Daddy!"

"Yes, my child, it is. Prepare for his home-call. It will come within a week."

Moni scarcely slept that night. She tossed and struggled, sure it couldn't be true. Next morning she arose earlier than usual and hastened home. She met her father at the gate. "You're early, my girl."

"Good morning, Daddy," she replied breathlessly. "Are you all right? Anything wrong with you?"

"Why do you ask?"

"A nasty dream. . . ."

He gave her a searching glance, then remarked, "Child, you can't place faith in dreams. Likely you ate something last night that didn't agree with you."

She laughed, and thankfully pushed the dream into her subconsciousness, but after breakfast Prosad called her. "Moni, my girl, can you spend a few minutes with me in the office?"

"Of course," she answered, and followed, wondering what was on her father's mind.

"I'm puzzled about some business matters, and I'd like your advice, my wise daughter," he began. He took the file of papers and explained everything carefully. They spent an hour together before a hasty glance at her watch showed Moni she'd be late for school if she didn't run.

Several days passed and Prosad's eldest forgot the dream. But five days later Moni walked home for breakfast as usual to find the verandah empty. Why wasn't Daddy waiting? She opened the office door to find him pacing the floor.

"What is it, Daddy? Aren't you well?"

"It's all right, Moni."

"Please, Daddy, tell me."

"No, child. Go and eat your breakfast."

"Daddy! You love me? Then tell me what's troubling you."

"All right, but go and eat first." Moni gulped her food, then rushed back to her father. He said, his voice hoarse with emotion, "My bank's failed. We're ruined financially, Moni. My bankers duped me."

"Does mother know?"

"I haven't told anybody yet, but your Uncle Sen knows it's unstable. He's a good man, Moni. You can trust him."

"Daddy! Don't worry with Uncle Sen. We'll manage on our own. We have my wages, and we can do it by adjusting." She looked at her wristwatch, then said, "I'll have to go, but I'll come back this afternoon, as soon as possible. Please, Daddy, don't worry. The Lord will care for us."

"Yes, daughter, go."

She rushed home after her last class, but Benoy met her on the road with, "Moni, Papa's very ill. Two doctors came."

She rushed into the house, pushing past the doctors while hearing them say, "Your father's condition is very serious, Miss," and on into the sickroom, where she took charge. "I'll stay, Mother," she said. "I'll call if there's any change."

"Thank you, Moni. I'm glad you've come," Kumdinni said and tiptoed out to Grandma and the other three children in the kitchen.

Moni leaned over the bed and said softly, "Daddy, I've come."

The man opened his eyes and whispered, "I'm glad. Jesus is calling me. I'm going home soon."

"Yes," she answered, "I know. He told me too."

"He did? When?"

"In the dream. Remember?"

"Love him always, Moni. He's waiting for you and me. Stay close to your Uncle Sen. He's a good man." Prosad sank back exhausted, then muttered, "The pain. . . ."

"Pray, Daddy. Jesus will heal it."

"He's real . . . so precious . . . Moni, I'm going!" The man sat up in bed, threw his arms around her neck, laid his head on Moni's shoulder and slumped. She suddenly heard herself say, "Lord Jesus, receive his spirit."

Leela, the youngest girl, came rushing in, sensing something unusual. "Call Mama, Leela," Moni said. "Daddy's fainted."

But Leela took a look at her father's face and said, "No, Moni, he's gone."

Her mother and grandmother unwound Prosad's arms from around Moni's neck and laid the body back on the bed. Moni, stunned, was sure he had only fainted. As Kumdinni and Grandma Duoya and the children began to wail, she slipped out to find the doctors. "Tell them he's just fainted," she said.

But the doctors confirmed Prosad's death, and suddenly Moni realized her father had left. She slumped to the floor in a faint, to awaken to the family's wailing as they huddled around her. Shocked into action, the new leader of this household arose and took charge, praying inwardly . . . please, Lord, your strength! For their sakes. . . .

"I must see Lawyer Sen Bannerjee immediately," she told the senior doctor. "Would you please find him for me?" He noted the address and left. "Grandma, do you know how to fix the body for burial?" Duoya nodded, and Moni added, "I'd like to help, but I should see about funeral arrangements. Mother, could you work with Grandma, after saying goodbye to the young doctor?"

"Of course, Moni."

Without an effort their roles had already reversed. Moni said quietly, "Dr. Kumar, please send your bill in my name, and I'll reimburse you. Mother will give you the address, and thank you for coming. Now, if all of you will excuse me, I'll go to Daddy's office. Send Uncle Sen to me there, please."

The dazed girl walked to her father's desk and picked up a scribbled message: "Moni," she read, "the battle continues. You must pick up my sword and wield it well. Lift the name of Jesus high. Let all hear. I die as a Christian, and I desire a Christian burial. My body must never be burned."

Prosad's daughter sat in her father's chair and wept. At last he had broken loose from the controls of Hinduism and was truly free. But in the hour of his release, he handed her the challenge to continue. She buried her head in her hands, then looked up and with arms raised, said, "Yes, Lord, it shall be so. I accept the sword."

That sacred moment changed the course of Moni's life. God had called through her father's note, and she could never be the same again.

For the next five years Moni sought the answer to one burning question: Where did the Lord desire her to wage the battle? Must she leave the security of the mission compound and go out on the front lines? Must she leave loved ones to touch those yet unreached by the gospel of Jesus Christ?

Her mother thought her mad. Kumdinni looked at her daughter and asked, "You're leaving a good job? For what?"

"I don't know, Mother. The Lord has called, and I must answer. He'll tell me as I obey."

"What has he called you to do?"

"To teach people who haven't yet heard the name of Jesus. There are millions in our country," she answered.

Kumdinni's lip quivered. "Moni," she said, "I've given in to your leadership. I know I have no further right to manage this home. Have you forgotten your family? What happens to us?"

"The Lord will meet your needs, even as he promises to care for me. Benoy has a good job and you and Leela can continue my embroidery trade that I've built since Daddy's death. Can't you manage, Mother?"

"Well, yes, but don't make hasty decisions. You're overworked. Take a month's vacation."

"Good idea. I believe I will," Moni replied.

That night she knelt longer than usual in prayer. "Dear Lord," she pleaded, "tell me where I'm to go. Which train? Which province? Which town?"

She dreamed, and there it was. She stepped off the train in a beautiful rural setting. She read the name on the platform sign: Sahibganj. To her right rolled a mighty river; to the left, verdant hills. The people spoke a mixture of Hindi and Bengali.

"What province is this?" she asked a bystander.

"Bihar," he answered, and she awakened.

"Bihar!" Moni exclaimed. "Thank you, thank you, Lord."

During that month's vacation, Prosad's daughter crisscrossed Bihar, always searching for Sahibganj. At last she found it, but not before she almost ran out of money. The young woman had purposefully tested the Lord by saying, "If you can't care for me this month, dear Lord, then you can't maintain me in the coming years."

During her travels she arrived late one night in an unknown town. Alighting onto the platform she prayed, "All right, Lord. What happens now? I have only one *rupee* in my purse."

A tap on her shoulder caused her to swing around to face an elderly Englishman with a kind face. "My wife is concerned about you, a young Indian woman traveling alone. She asked me to bring you over to meet her, and let us take you to our bungalow for the night."

Moni met the lady, and gratefully accepted their invitation. Before she left their home for Sahibganj, they insisted she take a gift to cover the rest of her journey!

Moni returned to Calcutta to resign as headmistress from the prestigious mission school attended by seven hundred girls. She now stepped out to battle darkness and ignorance in an area untouched by the gospel.

Lawyer Sen Bannerjee thought her rash. He shook his head and said, "You're crazy, Moni! How can you go unprotected to a place where you don't know anybody? And why are you leaving all your money here to care for your family? What are you going to live on?"

Her assurances barely reached him, but no amount of arguing changed her mind.

"Listen, Uncle Sen," she replied earnestly, "if Hindu holy men and women can take vows of poverty to seek salvation, can't a Christian *sanyasini* (religious woman mendicant) trust the true

God of heaven and earth? I know the Lord Jesus will care for all my needs."

In the fifteen years of fruitful ministry that followed, Moni proved God's faithfulness many times. She founded a mission called Dipti (Light) in Sahibganj, Bihar, beginning by teaching girls in a town that educated only boys. Her initial efforts expanded to teaching adults, then encompassed needy widows and orphans.

A true Indian mystic, Prosad's daughter stepped out in faith without any mission board, five-year-plan, personnel, or budget! Yet she moved with authority, getting her directives through intercessory prayer. Both Indian and European missionaries joined her as Dipti Mission spread to neighboring towns and regions.

How did she do it?

Known to the world as Prabhavati Sircar (the Christian name she embraced when she was baptized), Moni regarded her tryst with God as hallowed. She battled daily on her knees, and won victories that established Dipti Mission where there were no churches or any other Christian witness.

Prosad's daughter laid her sword down in 1941 when she answered her call home. The battle ended for both Prosad and his daughter, but they left many behind to continue fighting for Jesus.

*A shopkeeper selling gods and trinkets*

# Searching for the heartbeat of India

## Hinduism's claims

Both Sam and Arlene Zellers relished hot, spicy curries, Bengali sweets, and juicy *jalabies*. Ever since they had arrived in India three years prior to the day they crossed the Ganges, they became students of the land and its peoples. With some excitement they boarded the Asansol Northbound Express on a steamy April evening. Tomorrow morning they hoped to catch a treasured glimpse of India's soul!

The whirring fans and the monotonous click-click of the wheels on iron rails helped them sleep. Toward dawn people began stirring and soon the crowded train pulled slowly into the station at the river crossing, barely a quarter-mile from three waiting ferries.

Throaty cries filled the early morning air as doors pushed open to disgorge the train's impatient passenger load onto the sandy approaches. Frantic fathers sought family members, coolies shouted to clear obstructions from their path as they tottered toward the shore. No wonder, for each carried unbelievable loads of boxes and sundry on their heads! Men, women, and children wove in and out, each seeking advantage in their mad rush, motivated by the shrill whistles of the soon-departing ferries.

Their weary journey at an end, pilgrims sauntered about, glad for a chance to buy a hot meal at the busy little tea stalls bordering the route. Vendors sold trinkets, flowers and fruits for sacrifice, and daily needs. One could buy a toothbrush or comb as easily as pictures of Hindu gods and goddesses.

And in the waters of India's sacred river, Ganges, hundreds worshiped! They recited mantras, threw little boat-shaped baskets of stitched leaves bearing marigolds, rose petals, or Bengali sweets onto the flowing river. They drank of its holy waters, offered milk or curds, or stood facing the rising sun to cup their hands and three times let water slowly seep through as they offered it in libation to the sun. Hands joined in earnest petition, they remembered Shiva's promise as found in one of the ancient Puranas (compiled about 300 B.C.) that says:

"She [the Ganges] is the source of redemption. . . . Heaps of sin, accumulated by a sinner during millions of births, are destroyed by the mere contact of a wind charged with her vapour. . . . As fire consumes fuel, so this stream consumes the sins of the wicked. . . . Sinners who expire near the waters of the Ganges are released from all their sins. . . . They never die—not even on the day of the total dissolution of the universe."

Little wonder that with such promise, millions of Hindus follow the pilgrim trail to dip and bathe, to drink, to sacrifice, to cremate their dead, to throw the ashes onto those waters! There are longer rivers, wider, more beautiful ones in the world—but none as sacred!

The young missionary couple, coming from America, a world away, looked at the scene before them with wonderment. Under all the rushing and pushing would they be able to find something of value?

"I'll stay with the coolies," Sam said quickly as three uniformed porters wearing arm badges lifted the trunks and bedding rolls onto their heads. "Look for my red cap and shirt," he added.

Arlene, petite and plucky, nodded. She couldn't hope to keep up, but her athletic husband stood out clearly in the masses of not-so-tall Indians. Clutching her shoulder bag and their briefcase, she slipped through the crowds, always keeping that red hat and shirt in sight.

Just getting there gained new meaning! The three paddle wheel ferries, a quarter-mile away, whistled impatiently to motivate passengers. Arlene regretted not being able to stop. Fascinating facets of Indian life displayed themselves right here on the banks of the Ganges River, but the whistle and the sight of that red cap lured her on until both she and Sam had safely crossed the gangplank.

His blue eyes twinkled. "That's some crush, isn't it?" he commented, pushing his cap off his wet forehead to wipe his brow with a blue handkerchief. "Come," he said. "The coolies will stay with the luggage. We'll go upstairs."

Escape to the upper deck reserved for first-class passengers afforded the young couple reprieve, a delightful interlude in an otherwise harassing journey. A number of wealthy Indian families appropriated benches near the railings. White uniformed waiters scurried back and forth taking orders. One soon approached the Zellers and brought their order of eggs, tea, and toast on stainless steel tray, complete with cutlery, tea set and chinaware bearing the railroad seal. Arlene drew a deep breath. This too was India!

When Sam paid the bill he chuckled, having added a healthy tip for the waiter. "Honey, put that into dollars, and we've got cheap living here!"

She lifted troubled brown eyes to his and replied, "But we're not living on dollars. Didn't we leave them behind?"

What about the crush downstairs? Where would those passengers get food? She had learned enough to know that such utilized vendors, drinking hot tea from small earthen cups, discarded when used. A dip of potato curry with *chapatis* or delicious hot *purees* (forms of Indian bread) on several leaves stitched together sufficed. The villager doled out his hoarded *paisa* more cautiously than the privileged classes fingered a hundred *rupee* note! Some day, Arlene determined, she, too, would buy food from vendors. There must be some way to identify with the common people and still maintain normal health precautions!

A long, sharp whistle and the throb of engines accompanied the thrashing sound of the paddle wheel. The girl's train of thought broke as the ferry started maneuvering away from land. Sam grabbed his camera to snap a string of temples, each with its bathing steps and devotees. While bells clanged, white-robed priests chanted and worshipers bowed before Hanuman, Vishnu, Lakshmi, Ganesh, Shiva, Rama or some other preferred god or goddess. Within the broad spectrum of thirty-five million such deities, Hindus felt they most surely could find absolution somewhere!

Now the American photographer focused on a cremation site with one in progress. A small bullock cart stood nearby, loaded with fuel for the pyre. Four men had carried the corpse to the site and now sat several yards away. They were laughing and talking, in contrast to the principal mourner who lingered near the burning pyre. Was he grieving for father or mother, his wife, or child? Little matter! If he was a devout Hindu, he must have believed that in this cycle of reincarnations, his bringing his loved one to the sacred river, Ganges, had intercepted that long, irresolute route to take his departed one directly to "heaven." He had done the best he knew! Had he ever questioned, or did his mind now dulled by sorrow grasp whatever comfort he could find in tradition and legend?

The ferry chugged into mainstream and Sam photographed more cheerful subjects—a barge laden with men, bicycles and goats, some fishing boats. Fifteen minutes later, the crossing completed for the more than two-mile journey, pandemonium broke loose on the deck below.

Even before the gangplank was lowered, passengers pushed and yelled, seeking advantage to board the commuter train that awaited the ferry's arrival on the northern bank. Only the first would find seats!

Sam and Arlene descended into the middle of the seething mass. "Arlene, you go ahead and save a place. I'll come with the coolies," the tall, fair-haired American said.

Arlene nodded, then began moving with the crowd to escape injury. Out in the clear at last she hurried up the sandy beach to the waiting train. It would chug the seven long miles to the station where she and her husband would change to the mainline.

"Here, Memsahib!" somebody called in English. A young man leaned out a corner window and pointed to the open door of a compartment. "I need two places," the girl replied. He nodded, and she entered to find the compartment already well filled, all except the bench closest to the door. People pushed in, but Arlene spotted two empty places facing each other. She quickly appropriated one, then placed her feet on the opposite bench to reserve it for her husband.

A covered basket next to her shoe scarcely attracted the girl's attention. It looked ordinary enough, but the family to whom it belonged immediately became perturbed. Not until Sam arrived did the young couple learn their cause for anxiety.

The male members of the other family converged within moments of Sam's entrance. While the coolies stowed luggage in racks above and under the seats, a portly gentleman indignantly accosted Samuel Zellers. "Why have you disgraced our family god?" he cried.

The American missionary looked at him, uncomprehending. "Beg pardon, sir?" he said.

"My god is in that basket!" the man declared in anger. "Your wife has disgraced our god by placing shoe leather near!"

"Oh!" Arlene exclaimed, quickly removing her feet.

Her husband answered, "Please forgive us, sir. We didn't realize, but don't be so perturbed. The true and living God is much greater than this idol. He made the heavens and the earth."

"What?" the man shouted. "You also disgrace my god?" He began a loud tirade against the God of the Christians, declaring him to be no god. He stated his god's virtues, and affirmed him as all-powerful. The foreigners had dishonored his god! Now both he and his family would suffer.

Angrily the gentleman pulled off his clothes—his shirt, trousers, undershirt, money, watch! Rushing out in his shorts, he shouted back, "Now we'll see whose god is the true God!" The words wafted on the air as the gentleman hurried to the Ganges to wash away his defilement.

But within moments of that challenge the train whistle blew. The commuter began to move slowly, just fast enough to encourage the portly gentleman to try to get on. His sons and other family members hung out the open windows, cheering him on. Passengers joined in the shouting.

With the train gaining speed, the runner puffed and struggled to catch the caboose, but without success. One of the sons grabbed his father's clothes, money, and watch, and jumped off. Father and son would come hours later to rejoin their waiting family at the main station.

And what of Sam and Arlene Zellers? They sat without making comment, knowing that the Lord of heaven and earth was answering the challenge the man had given. God would do his own fighting!

When the hilarity subsided within the compartment, the ladies opposite the missionary couple took out their lunch basket. Instead of feeding the family, first they cared for their god . . . the god in the basket.

A five-inch porcelain idol sat on a small throne surrounded by dark red velvet. No doubt the family had paid a handsome sum at some pilgrimage location, and were taking the god home for proper installation in their worship room. There he would receive their daily offerings.

It was now lunchtime. The mother of this obviously wealthy Hindu family wiped the idol's face and hands, then held morsels of crumbled food to the figurine's lips. After a moment or two she laid the crumbs down and repeated the process, offering more.

The "meal" concluded, the woman again wiped the face of the little god. She straightened the red plush around the throne and replaced the lid on the basket. At last she could offer her family their lunch.

Had it been a small girl feeding her doll, the Americans would have smiled indulgently, but this experience shook them to the core. Could it be true? Did this woman, and millions like her, actually believe that a spirit resided within porcelain, clay, wooden, and other shapes? Even within photographs? Didn't reason tell them otherwise?

The missionaries sat mute, watching. So did the other passengers. When someone spoke, the voice was Indian, not heavy with a foreign accent. A man said boldly, "Huh! This isn't a god! What power does he have? He couldn't hold back the train! He couldn't eat his food! Now we know whose god is the true God. Now we know!"

Arlene and Sam glanced quickly at each other and smiled. Not only had they seen the Lord's victory, but in truth they had also glimpsed the empty soul of Hinduism.

## In a Muslim setting

Several years passed with Sam and Arlene Zellers spending much time pastoring in a nominal Christian community of Asansol. This important railway center, several hours north of Calcutta, boasted a sizable Anglo-Indian community peopled with families who called themselves either Anglican or Catholic, but who unfortunately knew little about a transformed life or true Christian witness. Sam often felt discouraged, nor did Arlene's too frequent attacks of malaria help. The Zellers longed and prayed for a spiritual breakthrough.

One evening toward the end of November Arlene thought her husband's footsteps seemed lighter than usual. She looked up from the couch and said with a smile, "Did it go better today?"

Sam threw his Bible and notebook onto the sidetable and answered, "Yes, honey, I have great news for you."

"Want a cold drink first? Dinner will be served at eight as usual."

"Thanks, that sounds good." The tall, fair-haired missionary sprawled in an easy chair. Looking around their attractive living room he noted its decor and furnishings, so like Arlene. His wife looked sweet in her blue and green cotton dress. Were they in India, or Kansas? Yet even as he pondered their propensity for things Western he heard the padded footsteps of the houseboy preparing the table in the dining room.

His wife called, "Bearer!"

A young man appeared and asked, "Yes, ma'am?"

"Bring the Sahib a cold glass of Campa Cola."

"Yes, your honor." With a nod he disappeared into the pantry.

"You had a busy day, dear?" she asked, hands behind her head.

"Calcutta's always tiring, especially with a committee meeting in the evening . . . but that's life."

"The church board again?"

"Yes, and you know, honey? I dare hope something's moving now. We're talking about an evangelistic outreach!"

"At last! You've been pushing them a long time, haven't you?"

"Too long. Ironically, now that they're steamed up, I'm not able to go. It conflicts with my teaching at the Bible School. Arlene, I hate to ask it, but. . . . " He paused as the bearer approached with a tray of cold drinks and finger food. They helped themselves, then dismissed the young man with a nod. Sam continued between bites, "As I was saying, honey, the board has decided on an evangelistic thrust, but the timing conflicts with my work here and my Bible teaching schedule in Calcutta."

"Can't they go on their own?"

He shifted, then said, "They want your accordion, Lena."

She looked up hastily. "I don't loan it out. You know that, Sam, and who would play it?"

"You, my dear. The team has chosen an area completely unchurched in a village section bordering Bihar. Dilip and Deepak are both ready to serve as evangelists, and they can handle magic lantern meetings at nights, but they want you, too."

"But the malaria. . . ."

Sam looked troubled, then said, "Pray about it. I know this is asking a lot of you, but if you can give three weeks to the tour it will strengthen the team. Deepak's wife will go as your helper with the women. I think it will work. We'll give you the small khaki tent so that you can get plenty of rest. Perhaps the mission in Ragnathpur will allow you to use their *shamponi*. That will make traveling to the villages easier."

"Hmmm . . . looks like it's all sewed up!" Arlene laughed and sat up. "When is the tour?"

"After the Christmas rush, when things slacken. You'd leave around the middle of January and run through the first week of February, before the hot west winds begin."

"But what will you do, Sam? How will you manage?"

"Just fine, honey." He chuckled, then concluded, "I told the committee I thought you'd consent. I hope I didn't presume . . . but honey, you know how much we've been praying for this. I wish I could go!"

"Never mind, dear. Next time!"

"I must go and clean up before dinner, but let me say just this. Sometimes, Arlene, I feel like leaving India! We're battling nominal Christianity here, just like in the States. Did we come for this?"

"Don't forget all the young lives you're touching. That's important." She drew a deep breath, then added, "When another door opens . . . or perhaps I should say, when the Lord opens another door, we'll enter."

For all her brave words the girl still felt some qualms as she packed her suitcase for the tour. What did she know about village India? Could she relate to those who had never heard the gospel? They would contact both Hindus and Muslims. Arlene prayed fervently, "I need your help, dear Lord. I feel so weak. How can I prepare?"

In answer to a definite urge, she tucked an English copy of the Koran into her reading materials.

Deepak and Ruma proved invaluable friends, especially when Arlene and Ruma tried visiting the women of the community. A few homes opened, but most remained closed. At the end of the first week the petite, dark-haired missionary began chilling with malaria. After the chills came fever. She was grounded until the quinine took effect. How could she spend her lonely hours in bed? Arlene read the Koran while Ruma continued visiting in Hindu homes.

Her particular quest centered on anything she could learn about Jesus. The Muslim holy book seemed new and fresh since she hadn't read from it in years. Finally, one week later, Arlene resumed day duty with Ruma, her friend.

This time they rode by *shamponi* to new villages north of the bazaar. They passed numerous settlements, finally one that displayed an impressive establishment next to a Muslim prayer place. Beyond was a Muslim village.

"Stop here," Arlene said to Joey, their faithful oxcart driver. "We'll try these homes."

They began knocking on closed doors, only to be denied, and as the day wore on Arlene's strength waned. Feeling weak and tired she turned to her companion. "Ruma," she asked, "why can't we get in?"

"Please forgive me, Memsahib," the little woman in the white *saree* responded, "but I think these folks consider you to be a man."

Arlene looked at her in amazement. "Ruma!" she exclaimed. "Whatever makes you think that?"

The little Bengali lady giggled, then said, "We're used to your dresses and pith helmet and glasses, but these people probably have never seen a white woman before. You don't mind my telling you?"

"Of course not, but I can't change now. I didn't think of wearing *sarees*. In fact, I have but one or two for special occasions."

They stood near the *shamponi* parked under a spacious mango tree. The village lay to their right, every door closed. "Lord, what shall I do?" Arlene prayed. "If we're to get in here, you'll have to open the door."

Just then a passerby stopped and exclaimed, "Good day, Memsahib! I didn't expect to see you here."

"How do you know me?" Arlene inquired.

"Of course I know you. You gave me good medicine at the mission dispensary in Asansol three years ago. You were helping an older lady."

Arlene smiled, remembering how she hated the job! "Yes," she said, "that was the Herr Missahib."

"Your medicine made me well. You didn't water it like the government dispensary does. You give good medicine."

The missionary's mind whirled. Was this man the Lord's answer to her prayer? Would he open the door? "Look, friend," she said, "these people seem to fear me. Since you know the mission and our work, perhaps you could introduce my friends and me. I'd appreciate that."

He smiled broadly and addressed himself to the bystanders who always congregated on any pretext. Today they saw a white woman wearing a dress, glasses, and pith helmet. Arlene Zellers flinched under such scrutiny.

The crowd pressed closer, and the man spoke, "Look, my brothers," he said, "I was ill and went to Asansol to the government hospital. But they did me no good. I stayed a week and paid lots of money, but didn't get well. Then I learned that they water down their medicines. Somebody told me about the clinic at the Christian mission. I went there and this lady gave me good medicine. You can trust her. She'll tell you the right way to live. She belongs to God's good people."

By this time at least sixty men, all Muslims, had gathered. Several carried a rope bed from a nearby house and placed it under a mango tree. "Please sit," they said to Arlene and Ruma, "and tell us what you want to say to our ladies."

Arlene lifted her heart in passionate plea to heaven, "Oh, Lord . . . more strength, please . . . and where do I begin?"

"Old Testament," came the swift answer.

She started with the creation story, even while her audience carefully scrutinized them. Two patriarchs, their white beards resting on their chests, sat directly in front of her. The others hovered around. Arlene began to smile as she thought. . . . Ah . . . Father Abraham, and Father Isaac, surrounded by their following. I wish Sam could see me now!

The narration moved from creation to such spiritual giants as the patriarchs, then to Moses, and King David. That led to the birth of Christ. "Now what, Lord?" Arlene inquired urgently.

"The Koran account. . . ."

She smiled at the listening group, seated on their haunches in a semicircle. "Let me tell you what the Koran says about the birth of Jesus, the Son of David," she began. "Did you know your scriptures describe it?" The men listened attentively. Not one responded, so she continued, "Friends, your holy book says that Jesus was born of the Virgin Mary under a coconut tree. It further details that a ripened fruit fell to nourish the mother, and the baby opened his mouth and said, '*Isa, Ruh, Allah!*'" (Jesus, born by the Spirit of God).

The men turned to the patriarchs. Was this true? Did the Memsahib know? One of them nodded and said, "Yes, she speaks the truth." His companion nodded and raised his right hand in affirmation.

Arlene continued, "I have read everything your Koran tells about Jesus, and I have also read everything the Holy Bible says. I find the Bible gives a much fuller account of his birth, life, and death, yes—and his resurrection. If you so desire, I'm glad to share my knowledge with your ladies, to give them a fuller understanding of Jesus. You know the Koran calls him the expression of the perfect will of God."

The elder brother spoke again, "She speaks the truth. She must come to my home first and meet all the ladies today."

The crowd rose and stretched, even while Arlene drew a deep breath. Apparently her day was not yet finished. "More strength, Lord! And thank you for guiding me."

"Memsahib," the patriarchs invited, "come with us. We're brothers and we live in that large group of houses you passed. Come and meet the women."

Ruma and Arlene trudged the hot, dusty road with all sixty men following. Flanked by the two leaders they made an interesting procession, one which caused Arlene to smile broadly as she wished fervently that Sam could see her now! "Who are they?" the Christian cartman asked one of the men in the crowd.

"Our *mulvis* (priests)," the man replied.

That began a witnessing session that continued long into the afternoon. The ladies sat on a rope bed in the open courtyard, and tittering, excited women appeared from everywhere—over fifty in number! Neither Arlene nor Ruma had ever known a more receptive audience, one that thoroughly enjoyed this unique interlude in an otherwise drab existence.

The sun had now passed its zenith and Arlene wondered how long her strength would hold. "Shouldn't you cook for your men?" she suggested after questions and answers had flown freely for over an hour.

"No, Memsahib," they said laughing. "We've waited a whole lifetime for you to come. Now that you're here, nothing else matters. The men can wait."

"All right, Lord," Arlene echoed in her heart. "Nothing else matters. More strength, please!"

The men plainly eavesdropped. At times the more curious parted the grass of the flimsy courtyard walls to see as well as to hear. Several evenings later the *mulvi* brothers invited the entire team to give an outdoor showing of the life of Christ to the whole Muslim community, to be followed by a sumptuous feast.

The door had flung wide open, nor did it close again. The elder brother procured a copy of the Bible and studied it avidly. Time and again he traveled quietly to talk to one of the older missionaries.

As for Arlene, once again she recognized a treasured glimpse into the hungry soul of India, this time among Muslims. How nearly she missed it, though, she reflected. It led to her packing away her dresses, discarding her pith helmet, and identifying more closely with her Indian brothers and sisters by wearing *sarees*, nor did she ever regret the change.

# The black book from God

Except for the granite mountain that overshadowed this strongly Hindu community, Kattapuram resembled any other in South India. The handbuilt pond drew worshipers to bathe in its waters prior to entering the shrine at the base of the peak. Here the devotees offered flowers, fruit, and curds to the idol.

In the shallower end of the pond, buffaloes wallowed in the mud while their young herdsmen, about six or eight boys, threw water on each other and shouted with delight. Women washed soiled linens at the bathing area, pounding them on bits of left-over brickwork from some former temple. They spread the clothes on bushes to dry, so that the torrid rays of the sun could draw out turmeric and curry stains.

Nearby, on the east bank, a magnificent mango tree provided shade for travelers, and became the site for village councils when day blended quietly into night. Some small brick dwellings with whitewashed walls and red tile roofs sought mutual solace, afraid to live apart. They huddled together, but gave way to one more courageous, a house that boasted a walled-in courtyard at the back and an iron gate in front. The town considered its owner important, none less than their local medical practitioner, Ranjit Ram.

Susheela, a young bride of sixteen, hurried to this house on a hot Tuesday afternoon. The girl's peasant-style full skirt swung around bare ankles and feet as she trod the hard-packed earthen trail past the local pond. Her hand-dyed red blouse matched the hibiscus flower tucked into her neatly combed hair, and over her shoulder hung the inevitable cotton bag that functioned as both pocket and basket. At this moment it carried the only copy of the Holy Scriptures in town, a Tamil New Testament.

Its owner read it regularly, ever since she learned of Jesus in the Mission Girls' School in Madras. Since Kattapuram educated only boys, Ranjit Ram chose to send his younger daughter to school to satisfy her desire for learning. After her recent marriage she had returned to live with her bridegroom a half-mile from her parents. Now Susheela sought an opportunity to share her faith in Jesus Christ with those whom she loved. She feared opposition, but took courage. Perhaps the Lord would give her a chance to witness today.

As it turned out, Mom was resting on a mat underneath the pipal tree in the back yard. Susheela plopped beside her and asked, "How's the fever? Better today, Mom? I was worried about you when I left yesterday."

The woman with greying hair smiled, then answered, "Oh, I'm all right, or I will be when the weakness goes. I had to work this morning. . . ."

"Oh, Mom, you should have called me."

"But Susheela, you have your own duties, and you must remember to please your husband. He's your lord."

"Well, yes, Mom, but I could have come earlier. I can arrange the work pretty much as I like since I have to run the home. With the younger boys in boarding school in Madras and Muthu's widowed mother with her daughter, my days are pretty much my own. Anyway, Mom, you rest now while I keep an eye on the grains."

She waved her arm toward rice sunning on several mats. The older woman nodded and yawned. Turning over on her side, she soon slept. Susheela drew the black book from her bag and began to read.

Half a mile away, Susheela's father, Ranjit Ram, strolled out of his local clinic into the nearby marketplace. He glanced at his watch and noted the express bus should arrive soon. Meandering over to the General Store he greeted his friend, the proprietor. Groups of men began to converge on this popular meeting place. Meanwhile, two decrepit busses stood waiting. Passengers milled around the various tea stalls, sharing gossip.

The Express came in with a flourish to screech to a halt near the General Store. Passengers poured out, seeking a hot lunch at one of the many tea stalls while vendors carried their wares into the vehicle to service those who preferred keeping their seats to standing for the rest of the journey. Seats were never held, except by occupancy!

An observer would have noted the predominance of men. Women, if any, stayed discreetly out of sight. In this land the sexes seldom mingled. Even in the marketplace the man had right-of-way.

But in the providence of God, it was the women who first heard the gospel in Kattapuram. When Susheela's mother, Shanti, stirred to find her daughter reading with absorption, she sat up and exclaimed, "Susheela! What are you studying?"

Shanti glanced suspiciously at the girl, aware of a glow on her face that defied explanation. She rose and grabbed the volume from her daughter's hands. Shanti opened it, wishing she could read.

Susheela looked up, then said, "Mom, don't get angry. It's a book from God. I've read many books in school in Madras, but never any like this one. This is different."

"How? What makes it different?"

"It tells about God."

Shanti sniffed, then asked, "God? Which god? Lord Shiva, Venkateshwar, Vishnu? Ram? Is it about them? Tell me!" The mother squatted opposite her daughter, demanding an answer.

"None of these, Mom. This tells about the Lord Jesus."

"Lord Jesus? I know Lord Krishna, but who is Jesus?"

"He's quite unlike our gods," the girl replied. She took the book from her mother and flipped the pages. "This tells about his life. See? Here's a picture of his birth. The story is on the other side of the page."

"He's not Indian! Look, his face is white!"

"No matter, Mom. He came from heaven for the whole world, so his birth took place in the middle of East and West. Would you like me to read for you?"

The older woman sat back against the tree trunk and grunted, then warned, "Read exactly what it says. I want to know whether it's good or bad."

"Yes, of course."

Mother and daughter spent an hour perusing the contents of the New Testament that Susheela had brought from the big city. The older woman listened intently, occasionally asking a question, but mostly absorbed in watching the glow on her daughter's face.

"See, Mom?" Susheela concluded. "It's a good book, a very precious book. Can you believe it? The Lord Jesus loves all of us, even the little children! And didn't you like that story about the woman at the well? I did."

Shanti answered slowly as she passed her right hand over her closed eyes, "I'm glad you read, daughter. I feel better now." She drew a deep breath and nodded, smiling.

"That's wonderful, Mom! I'll do it again tomorrow. Do you think Jyotsamma would like to listen?"

"You can ask her."

Not only did Jyotsamma join her mother and younger sister in the reading sessions, but she told her friend, Premi.

"Could I listen?"

"I'll find out," Jyotsamma answered.

Susheela glowed upon hearing the request. "Of course!" she exclaimed. "This book is for everyone. Tell all the ladies."

Next morning at the village well Premi announced, "We're going to hear Susheela read from a precious book she's brought from Madras."

"What kind of book?" a girl next to her asked.

"One that's come from God."

"Really? What's it like?"

"We'll tell you tomorrow morning."

Next morning Jyotsamma and Premi said excitedly, "Ever hear of living water? Susheela read about the Lord Jesus offering a woman living water!"

"Where? Where?" Four ladies converged to hear more.

"Come this afternoon when all the men go to the market square to meet the Express bus. We can ask Susheela to read it to us again this afternoon."

This led to daily reading sessions with more and more ladies finding excuses to wander over to the walled-in courtyard of Ranjit Ram's home. They became women of the Book. Their thirst for Bible study drew them to an English missionary lady living some three miles to the west in a small mission compound. She already had a full assignment caring for orphans, but "Sister Suzy" (as they called her affectionately) arranged special afternoon meetings for the ladies. One by one they took baptism, declaring faith in Jesus Christ. Sister Suzy organized them into the

Andrew Band, helping to nurture them in the faith. And all the while, the men knew nothing of this spiritual life movement! But one day the picture changed.

On a blazing hot Tuesday afternoon, with neither man nor beast likely to stir, the sexton of the little mission church rang the bell for service. Reverend Samuel, the Indian evangelist, arose from his knees after praying earnestly for the Spirit's anointing. Despite the breeze that blew in his open window, he dreaded the exertion ahead of him. Yet, as he entered the church he faced eighty village women, all dressed in colorful *sarees*, their faces filled with expectancy. The grey haired preacher felt ashamed of his lethargy and prayed inwardly, "Forgive me, Lord. Pour your word through me, lest I disappoint these eager listeners."

The voices of the women rose with fervor as they sang to the accompaniment of the little pump organ Sister Suzy played. Their spontaneity in prayer and obvious joy in worship struck the preacher as totally different from any congregation he had known. Reverend Samuel preached in great power, and many responded to his invitation.

At the conclusion of the service the guest turned to his missionary friend and asked, "Who are these women?"

The fair-haired, blue-eyed lady with the lilting soprano voice replied, "Padre Sahib, these are my friends, all women of the Book. I'll tell you the story over our cup of tea."

With a nod he left the church to walk over to the bungalow, only to find one of the women awaiting him. She pulled her *saree* shyly over her head, then said softly, "Please, Brother Samuel, my husband desires to talk with you privately. I've been witnessing to him, and he believes in Jesus. He wants to be baptized."

"Is that so? Why, sister, that's wonderful! Tell him I can see him at ten o'clock tonight, if that's satisfactory."

"Yes, pastor," she said.

Shortly before the arranged hour the evangelist slipped into the darkness to meet his guest. He sniffed the fragrance of jasmine on the hot, humid air. The stars above shone clearly and a wisp of moon hung in the heavens. In the stillness of that South Indian night, the preacher drew a deep breath and prayed fervently for discernment and guidance.

Within a matter of moments a cyclist approached. "You're the Padre Sahib?" the man asked.

"Yes," Samuel acknowledged, "and you?"

"I'm Ishwar Doss, owner of the General Store in the bazaar. You met my wife this afternoon."

"Park your cycle here inside the gate, and let's walk on down the lane. . . . What a beautiful night!"

They walked in silence, then the evangelist prompted, "You wanted to see me? May I help you?"

"Yes, Padre Sahib. From the time my wife mentioned your coming I determined to meet you." He turned to his companion and said, "You, see, I believe in Jesus."

"What do you mean, believe? Tell me your story, friend."

"I'm not what you call a religious man," he began. "To please my parents I went on several pilgrimages, took a vow or two, and gave alms to beggars, but it doesn't mean anything."

"Then?" prompted the preacher. "Usually we have to come to the end of ourselves before we begin searching, don't we?"

"How did you know?" Ishwar Doss stopped and looked at his companion in amazement. They stood near a pile of rocks that appeared strangely grotesque in the wan moonlight. The wail of a stray jackal rose from a clump of palms beyond the rice fields. The shopkeeper shuddered and said, "It reminds me of another night . . . when our eldest son died of cholera. That hit me hard. Then our second child died at birth, but his mother lived. I felt the gods were against me."

"You carried a heavy burden, friend."

"I did, Padre Sahib, until I met Jesus. Now he's changed my life. I love him, and I desire baptism. Will you do it for me?"

"Do you attend the mission church?"

"Oh, no! That's for Christians! I've never been inside."

"Then how did you hear about Jesus Christ?"

"My wife told me. You see, she's completely changed in the last six months. She used to worry me for money, and had a terrible temper . . . not any more!"

"A good exchange, I'd say," the preacher commented with a smile.

"But I can't tell you what it did to me! I beat her, kicked her, determined to make her angry again. Her sweetness and submission made me madder yet, but finally I gave in and asked her secret."

"Yes?"

"She told me about Jesus, and the black book from God the ladies have in their possession. Together we prayed for the forgiveness of my sins, and I'm a new man. It's wonderful, Padre Sahib. Won't you baptize me?"

"Tomorrow morning at five o'clock. Will you come?"

"Yes, I'll be here, regardless of consequences."

The baptism took place in the lake nearby with only a handful of Christians and a stray boy or two watching. But the news spread through the bazaar like dry tinder on fire, "Ishwar Doss has become a Christian!"

"How?"

"He went through a water ritual," the informant announced. "My son saw it!"

"You don't say," Ram Singh, the town clerk shouted. "We'll boycott the store. We'll thrash him!"

He rushed home, enraged. He could scarcely talk. "What is it?" his wife asked. "Come," she urged, "eat your breakfast, Ram, and be decent. I've never seen you like this before."

"Shut your mouth, woman! What do you know?" he sputtered, then added, "Sohan Lal's son saw Ishwar Doss become a Christian! He can't get away with that! We'll boycott him."

"Oh?" she answered quietly. "And what will you do with me, your wife? I'm a Christian, a member of the little mission church."

"What?" he yelled, giving her a mighty blow. She cringed, but stood up again. "Beat me if you like, but let me tell you that I'm not the only Christian around here. There are seventy-nine others, eighty with Ishwar Doss!"

Ram Singh stopped short. "You're lying," he yelled.

"No, I'm not lying. You men have more on your hands than you realize. If you deal harshly with Ishwar Doss, you must first take care of your wives."

The man dashed out the door. He rushed to the bazaar and spread the news. Soon the seventy-nine men dragged their wives to the Hindu temple. They came en masse.

"Bow!" each man commanded his wife, but the women made no move.

"Bow to the idol, or I'll thrash you!"

Instead, the women lifted their hands in prayer. Tears streamed down their cheeks as they felt the lashes, but not one recanted. Susheela cried, "Forgive them, Lord Jesus, and deliver us. Let them meet you, O God."

The men renewed their efforts, but not one woman gave in. Finally they turned home, sullen and beaten by some power greater than themselves. But the women stayed and prayed, "Now, Lord, do the rest. You have begun a good work, and we know you'll finish it." With bruised bodies but joyful spirits, they sang their way home.

Ten days later Ram Singh, leader of the opposition, went insane. He kept babbling, "Help the Christians build a church . . . help the Christians build a church . . . help the Christians build a church. . . ."

One year later, on invitation, Reverend Samuel returned for meetings in the new church in the village. The joyous congregation met him in a victory march—in their hands, palms, and songs of joy on their lips. The black book from God had done its work.

# In behalf of Lukhi

The anxious young mother ran to the group of small children playing at the end of the lane of Santal houses. "Have you seen my Lukhi?" she inquired.

A little girl with tousled hair and dancing black eyes looked up from making mud pies. "No, auntie," she replied, "not since she didn't feel well. She said her head hurt."

"How long ago?" Rita asked, tilting little Pakku's face upward so she could look deep into her eyes.

The girl swept her arm toward the horizon. "When the sun was about there," she said.

"Thank you, Pakku," Lukhi's mother answered. A frown covered her naturally pleasant features. She walked the length of the lane, glancing right and left. How had her daughter hurt her head? Had she fallen?

Several women watched her with interest. They were chatting casually, seated on the two-foot ledges that adorned each house, built to invite the weary to rest, or the lonely to find a friend. Two rows of neat dwellings, whitewashed and clean, bordered the one lane the village boasted. Lukhi surely couldn't have wandered far, Rita mused.

"Probably went to the field to her father," an older woman suggested with a half-sneer and a toss of her head.

"No," Rita muttered, shrugging her shoulders and walking quickly to her own courtyard. What made Kalyani so nasty? Was she a witch? Everybody knew a little girl of five wouldn't go to the field on her own. And besides, little Pakku said Lukhi had hurt her head.

*North Bihar Santal woman and child*

She turned into the courtyard belonging to her father-in-law. Three houses surrounded the common courtyard, but today all were empty since the family had gone to market. Only Rita and Lukhi remained to watch the grains drying in the sun. Lutu, Rita's husband, was in the field.

"Lukhi, Lukhi!" Rita called. "Where are you, darling? Come quickly, little one."

No answer.

The mother squinted in the bright sunlight, walked to the back of the three houses and approached the well. Fear gripped her . . . perhaps? She peered into the brackish waters, but saw no sign of the child. Thankfully, she turned back.

The hut! She had given just a hasty glance, not anything more. But if Lukhi's head hurt, she would want to lie down. Perhaps she had slipped in unnoticed while her mother spread the grains on the mats.

"Lukhi," Rita called as she stepped into the hut. She stopped, trying to accustom her eyes to the darkness. A slight movement caught her attention and a moan escaped the lips of the child huddled on a grass mat in the corner. Her mother quickly bent over the girl.

"Lukhi, darling," she said, touching the girl's arms, "what's the matter?"

The girl winced and drew back. "Please, Ma, don't hurt me."

"You're feverish. Is something wrong?"

"These little beans."

"Beans? What beans?"

"All over my body, Ma."

"Come into the light, child. Let me see you."

She helped the whimpering girl to her feet and brought her into the sunlight on the verandah. Welts had risen all over her body. Lukhi's face contorted in pain.

"Go, lie down on the bed, Lukhi. Your father will come for his noon meal soon, and I'll tell him. He knows about medicine. You'll soon be well, little one."

"Some water, Ma," her daughter pleaded. Rita ran to the earthen pot at the corner of the verandah, and taking a dipper of the cooling liquid brought it back to the child. The girl drank eagerly and her mother said, "Let me help you back to your father's bed. He'll come soon, and you'll be all right when he gives you medicine."

Lukhi lay down on the one bed the family possessed. Her mother forced herself to start the noon meal but her thoughts churned as she prepared vegetables and ground spices.

That Kalyani, she thought. I'm sure she's a witch . . . hmm . . . maybe the cause for this illness. She hasn't been nice to us since we became Christians! Didn't Soma tell me? We've had one sort of trouble or another ever since we were baptized . . . but Lutu won't recant! When will he see we've angered the evil spirits by forsaking them?

Rita ground the spices angrily, dashing a little water on them, then mixing turmeric with the garlic and onions she had crushed. She placed the iron pot on the earthen stove outside, blew on the embers, and fanned them furiously into a flame by adding twigs and leaves. The flame leaped up, its fingers reaching out from under the pot like some evil thing desiring to mar their family life. Rita shuddered.

Out in the cornfields beyond the village, Lukhi's father, Lutu, mopped his brow. He began his day early and worked until the torrid heat of the sun forced him to stop. Now he faced homeward for his noon meal and afternoon rest. About three o'clock he would return to finish his day's labors in the cool of the waning sun.

Lutu, tall and strong, was a man of few words. Instead of gossiping, he spent many hours praying as he plowed and planted, then later harvested his crops. He had worked hard, and his corn flourished. Perhaps he would have a good yield this year, the first since he had confessed faith in Jesus Christ. The man raised his heart in prayer today as he left the field to return home for lunch and a well-earned rest.

But Lutu found an anxious wife awaiting him. Lukhi tossed with high fever and moaned in pain. "Do something!" Rita pleaded with her husband.

"I'll try," he answered patiently. He administered what first aid he knew, but Lukhi's fever continued throughout the day and far into the night.

The mother kept vigil, hardly finding time to sleep. Next morning she said aloud, "Why all this trouble? What's the use of praying?"

"Rita!" the man said in amazement, "Surely you don't mean that! Of course there's use in praying. I've done all I know to do, but we could call Pastor James to anoint Lukhi with oil and pray. Jesus heals, you know."

"Do you believe that?"

"Yes! Don't you?"

She hesitated. Her husband didn't notice as he hurried off to call the pastor.

"Will she recover today?" Rita asked when Pastor James concluded the anointing service. But even with the question the young woman glanced quickly toward the corner of the hut where she had hidden fetishes to evil spirits. Lutu's wife demurely followed Pastor James out of the sick room and heard him affirm, "Lutu, don't worry. Your daughter will get well soon. Our Lord is faithful!"

Throughout the day Lukhi's mother hovered near the sick child, watching for signs of recovery, but none came. Three days later the parents noticed Lukhi's strength had almost gone.

"I don't understand this," Lutu said with a puzzled frown. "We believe in Jesus, and we trust him. I know he wants to heal Lukhi. Are you praying, Rita?"

"Of course I'm praying," the young woman answered shortly.

"To Jesus?" Lutu searched the woman's face.

"Why do you ask?" she retorted. She rose from the bedside mat and walked over to the door to begin preparations for their evening meal. Not that either parent ate much these days, but they must have enough strength to meet the demands of their twenty-four-hour vigil. Lutu had given up working in the field to aid his wife at the bedside.

Lukhi's father took his place on the mat beside the bed. He gently soothed the tossing child and prayed again for her healing. She relaxed, so he thought she slept. The man turned a troubled face to Rita and said, "Something is wrong. I don't see you interested in spiritual things like you were last year. We never pray together any more. Your work seems so important. Are you sure you love Jesus above all else?"

"Huh!" The young woman straightened after taking some potatoes from the bag. Her black eyes flashed as she retorted, "Who do you think I am? A witch?"

"Please, Rita," her husband begged, "don't talk like that. We left evil spirit worship last year and turned our backs on Satan."

"Then why doesn't God heal our daughter? I ask you, is Satan stronger than God?"

The man mopped his brow, then answered quietly, "Lower your voice, Rita. We can't afford to fight. Our daughter's life depends on our being true to God and to each other right now. Rita, tell me, please . . . do you love Jesus?"

"I used to," she said, eyes seeking refuge from Lutu's searching glance.

"And now?"

"My friend Soma told me the spirits are stronger. She gave me some fetishes to keep sickness and bad luck away."

The man drew back, surprised. "Fetishes? In this house?"

"Yes, Lutu. You can believe in Jesus and I'll believe in the spirits. Then one or the other of us will be right."

"Rita! You don't realize what you're saying!"

The sick girl began to toss and moan, and her mother quickly knelt by the bed. "What is it, Lukhi darling? Tell me."

"Jesus, Jesus! Not the spirits, Mama!"

"Oh, she overheard!" The woman broke into tears, weeping uncontrollably at the bedside. "Oh, God, forgive me. Am I the cause of Lukhi's illness? Lord Jesus, forgive!"

Her husband lifted her up quietly, and said, "Come outside, Rita. I'll get Grandma to stay with Lukhi for awhile."

An hour later Rita's friend, Soma, clasped her bundle closer and tiptoed around the corner of Lutu's house. A silver moon rode above the horizon. The evening was quiet and warm, but from the nearby mango tree Soma heard someone weeping. She followed the sound to find Rita lying on a mat on the ground.

"What's wrong, Rita? Is it Lukhi? Did she die?"

"No, but she's much worse. Lutu and Grandma are with her now to give me a little relief."

"Well, dry your tears. Lukhi's going to get well fast. See? I've brought you a magic potion." She opened her bundle and drew out a bottle. "Just rub some of this on Lukhi when nobody is near and I'll teach you the words to say. It's a powerful mantra (incantation). I guarantee your daughter will get well."

Rita sat up, bracing herself against the tree. She cried out in terror, "No, no, Soma! I'm the cause for Lukhi's illness. I should have said no when you first approached me."

"Don't be silly," her friend said, seating herself on the mat beside Rita. "How could you cause Lukhi's illness when you're worshiping the spirits? They only fight those who are against them. You're just too tired to think. Here, Rita, take the potion, and I'll teach you the words."

But Lukhi's mother recoiled. "No!" she whispered, hands on her friend's shoulders. "No!"

"But you love your child, don't you?"

"Of course."

"Then why can't you help her get well?"

"I've given myself to Jesus again, and I'm going to trust him. I've left the evil spirits!"

"You foolish woman! Your daughter is too sick for you to play with a foreign religion. You're a Santal! Your own religion is reliable."

"No, no, Soma! You don't understand. The spirits obey Satan, God's enemy. I'm sorry I took those fetishes from you. I'm done with Satan and all his works."

"So? And now he's stricken your daughter? Tell me, who's stronger?"

Her sharp laugh rang out, but Rita turned to look at her companion and said earnestly, "Listen to me, Soma. My daughter loves Jesus, and so does my husband. But I became cold toward him. Now he's punishing me."

"What slavery!"

"You don't understand. Jesus loves me, and our family belongs to him. When I turned from his love, how else could he get my attention? I'm afraid he's going to take Lukhi home to heaven, but if he does, it's all right. She'll be with him, where she can never get sick again."

"You traitor! What kind of mother are you?" Soma got up, grabbed the potion and stalked away. But sudden peace overwhelmed Rita, the peace she had missed for months.

She slipped into the sickroom, walked to the corner and drew out the fetishes hidden in the rafters. The embers outside still glowed under the pot of curry Grandma had cooked. Lukhi's mother threw the fetishes, bits of sticks and feathers, into the fire. The sudden flame, sizzle, and pop pronounced their end. Finished with evil spirits!

Rita smiled, a celebration of victory. She entered, and her husband noticed a difference. He touched her hand. She whispered, "Yes, Lutu, I did it. They're gone! Now we belong to Jesus. He can take our daughter if he wishes, but I have peace."

On midnight of the sixth day Lutu and Rita watched their daughter sink lower and lower. The man slipped out and faced the heavens. "Lord Jesus," he prayed, arms lifted up, "we know you are watching over us and we thank you. We belong to you. The villagers know this, but they're watching to see if Lukhi will die. For the sake of your witness in our village will you please heal her? Dear Lord, show this people your victory over Satan."

He sensed assurance, and with a smile the young father again took his place at Lukhi's bedside. "Go to sleep, Rita," he said. "It will be all right. I'll keep watch." But his weariness overcame him, and placing his head on the wooden bed frame, Lutu slept.

In his dream a venerable old man approached him and asked, "Lutu, do you believe in Jesus?"

"Yes, sir."

"Do you believe that Jesus Christ is God?"

"Yes, sir, with all my heart."

"Do you believe he will heal your child?"

"I know he will."

"Then cover every part of her body with dust. Do it in the name of Jesus, and she will live."

As the first streaks of dawn began to tint the eastern sky, Lutu awoke. He sat up dazed, stricken to think he had slept, but a quick scrutiny showed that Lukhi was still breathing lightly. It was as though her frail spirit merely hovered to say farewell. But Lutu had the Lord's promise!

He looked around for Rita. She had already risen, and was outside on the verandah struggling to light the fire under the little stove. He must move without her. Stooping over his daughter he gathered her in his arms and started for the door. Rita saw her husband carry the frail body out of the house and into the courtyard. What had happened? Had Lukhi died? If so, why hadn't Lutu called her? And why would he take her outside? People always prepare a body inside for burial. . . .

She could scarcely formulate words. She rushed over, her face drawn with anxiety. "Lutu!" she whispered. "What is it? Has she gone? Why didn't you tell me?"

He smiled, even as the girl groaned. "No, Rita," he answered. "Don't worry. You and I know the Lord is going to heal her. I just have a little job to do. The Lord gave me directions."

"But where are you going?"

"Come and see."

They laid their daughter on the ground, and the man began to cover every part of her body with dust. Over and over, even as he worked, he said, "Be healed in the name of Jesus, Lukhi. Be healed."

The ritual accomplished, Lutu lifted the girl again in his arms and carried her back to bed. Rita followed. Within moments the woman whispered excitedly, "Look! She's sleeping."

"The Lord has done it, even as he said he would."

"Oh, praise God! Praise God!"

That paean of praise continued in that little hut during the next two hours while Lukhi slept. When the girl awoke, her parents rejoiced to hear her say, "Mama, I'm hungry."

The woman bent over the girl, then exclaimed, "Look, Lutu! The lumps have gone. Her skin is clear!"

The girl sat up and reiterated, "Please, Ma, I'm starved. Is breakfast ready?"

Rita laughed aloud, even as she heard the cooing of doves and the chattering of sparrows in the courtyard trees. All nature is singing God's praises, she mused as she answered, "Yes, darling, your breakfast is ready. Your father and I have eaten, but we kept yours for you."

Lukhi's mother felt her heart would burst. She turned to Lutu and said, "I can hardly wait to tell Soma. She must hear what the Lord has done for us!"

# Jisu Muni's request

Govind Ram, owner of Purnea's largest cloth store, chuckled as he sat crosslegged on a platform covered with white muslin. Half a dozen *saree* lengths lay opened around him. On a bench drawn up to the platform an elderly pink-turbaned gentleman fingered a flowered silk *saree*. The voice of a foreign lady speaking on the street outside sounded clearly. She spoke Hindi fluently with scarcely any trace of accent, although her tonal inflection proclaimed her a Westerner.

Govind Ram peered out the door and said pointing, "Jisu Muni. She comes at least five times a week."

His customer let the folds of the rich silk *saree* fall while he looked and asked, "What is she doing?"

"Preaching about Jesus," his informant said with another hearty chuckle. "See those young fellows? They pretend interest . . . to keep her speaking. Really, she's very amusing."

"Maybe they are, too," the lawyer said with a smile. "Young people seem to enjoy novel types of entertainment, even at the expense of others." He picked up a dark red *saree* and started examining the floral pattern. "I think she would like this," he muttered. "Roses are her favorite flowers." Then he looked up and asked, "You called the foreigner 'Jisu Muni'—Jewel of Jesus. Why?"

The rotund and balding shopkeeper shifted his lotus-like position and said with a broad grin, "What else? You can't meet the lady without her talking about Jesus."

68

"I see . . . but why make fun of her? After all, here in India we have religious mendicants who take vows of chastity and poverty. Do we laugh at them? Perhaps this good woman has suffered much to live here."

"Why do you think so?"

"I got my advanced training in the West, and you wouldn't believe the luxurious living they enjoy. Why should anyone want to leave and come here?"

Govind Ram gave his customer a quick look. "Hmmm . . . never thought much about it. We just enjoy laughing at the foreigner, but I must say she speaks beautiful Hindi. Maybe I'll buy one of her Scriptures one of these days. She carries them in her shoulder bag."

The elderly gentleman rose, saying, "I'll return tomorrow if I don't find anything I like better than this last one." He went out and joined the crowd around the street preacher.

He judged her to be in her fifties, living simply. Her white cotton dress fell to within a foot of the ground. Strong leather sandals, obviously foreign, covered her bare feet. She wore a pith helmet to shield herself from India's merciless sun and, indeed, her shoulder bag bulged with literature. At the moment the bag hung from the handlebar of her bicycle she had propped against the trunk of the tree under which she stood. Her face glowed with earnestness.

"My brothers," she cried, "listen to me! God sent me to you. He wants you to turn from your idols and your sin. He loves you! Salvation is yours, not through bathing in the waters of the Ganges, but by believing on Jesus, God's only son."

Someone tittered, "So God's only son is Jesus. There she goes . . . talking about Jesus again . . . Jisu Muni!"

A college student called out, "How can we believe on Jesus unless we hear about him? Tell us more."

Elizabeth Liechti, a Swiss missionary living in Purnea, North Bihar, turned eagerly to the questioner. Her eyes glowed as she answered and a ripple of mirth spread through the entire male audience. The elderly lawyer heard the young man say to his friends, "Easy to get her started, isn't it? But where did she get that beautiful Hindi?"

Cyclists rang their bells as they skirted the crowd. Pedestrians loitered, then left with a laugh. Trucks and busses blared their horns even while Jisu Muni once again recounted the matchless story of God's love for sinful man. Then she moved on, to stop at another likely spot and repeat the process. At the end of many more such sessions she cycled home to meet her fellow missionary, Lilly Ammon. Their two-roomed bungalow always proved a haven from heat, noise, and city grime. Elizabeth parked the cycle on the verandah, then went in to meet Lilly, her junior by about five years.

"That you, Elizabeth?" a lilting voice called from the back verandah over the hissing of the pressure stove. The smell of curry filled the air and the weary newcomer smiled.

"Yes, Lilly." She threw her shoulder bag down, then on second thought picked it up and hung it on its hook behind the door. Lilly, the careful housekeeper, would never allow anything to remain out of place in these small quarters. Elizabeth walked onto the back verandah, drew a deep breath and said, "Sure smells good!"

Lilly wiped her perspiring face with a hand towel, then pushed her curly light brown hair off her forehead. Her open features and engaging smile made Lilly friends wherever she went. Now she asked, "How did things go today, Elizabeth?"

"Not too well. Plenty of chances to preach, of course, but I always feel it's useless. The crowd doesn't take me seriously . . . just wants me to amuse them." Her shoulders sagged, and lines of tiredness clung to her features.

"Nonsense! Your Hindi is ever so much better than mine," her friend consoled. "You speak earnestly. I know they'll remember what you say."

"I wonder sometimes. There was one man . . . older . . . wearing a pink turban. He seemed serious, and he encouraged me. God bless him." She asked, "Now, what about you? How was your day?"

"So-so."

"What did you do?"

"Scrubbed hospital floors and cleaned bathrooms."

"No, Lilly! Don't they hire sweepers for that?"

"Of course, but no hospital in Switzerland would ever consider using such a filthy place as this hospital in Purnea. I've taken all I can. So today I asked the lady doctor for vacation, and then I spent my time scrubbing!"

Elizabeth laughed. "Didn't you shock everyone?" she asked.

"Believe me, they thought I was mad!" Lilly grinned, and added, "A white woman on her knees, washing the floor with antiseptic solution? Pure, downright crazy!"

Her companion chuckled and the weary lines receded. "So you washed floors while I preached on street corners! We're sure different."

By this time Lilly had turned off the stove, emptied the curry into a stainless steel bowl and carried it to the small card table set for two right inside her bedroom door. She added hot *chapatis* (Indian bread) covered to keep soft, and filled the glasses with distilled water from the filter in the corner of the verandah. The two ladies sat, Elizabeth asked the blessing, and the conversation continued as they ate.

Lilly began, "Remember when I used to accompany you each day? I felt so useless and out of place. Now I don't."

The older woman said earnestly, "I'm so glad we prayed this thing through. The Lord showed me you had the gift of helps, and I the gift of evangelism."

"I certainly can't preach."

"But your gift speaks louder than mine," Elizabeth added as she attacked some curry with a bit of *chapati*."

"Why? I don't think so."

"Yes, Lilly, people appreciate the gift of helps. Something happens, something positive. You had a clean floor and a natural witnessing situation, but in my work. . . ."

*Elizabeth Liechti*

Her companion asked, "But don't the crowds come? You never lack for listeners."

"Lilly! I preach my heart out while they egg me on so that I can amuse them. I think that's terrible!"

"It is, Elizabeth, and after we finish eating, let's pray about it."

That prayer session brought forth some unusual results.

Five hundred miles west of Purnea, a famous religious fair met in Allahabad at the joining of two sacred rivers. Hundreds of thousands of pilgrims packed all incoming trains. Many sought peace and forgiveness of sins. The majority, however, probably considered this a vacation, time to visit relatives and friends. To such, the bathing rites meant barely fulfilling a ritual. Once accomplished, they spent the remainder of their time in the hastily constructed bazaars and amusement centers.

To meet the annual influx, the city of Allahabad stocked heavily in foods, trinkets, medicines and games of chance for the shanty town that mushroomed on the banks of the Yamuna. A festive air pervaded the *mela* with loudspeakers blaring.

But one religious mendicant stood knee-deep in water, hands folded as he worshiped the rising sun. For him this journey spelled one more attempt to free his conscience of the guilt that haunted him. How could he know forgiveness and obtain assurance of salvation? He had traveled throughout India, with always one more holy place beckoning. To what end? The gnawing emptiness remained! If only his parents could return from the dead to forgive him the wrong he committed against them.

The *sadhu* bathed where the river Yamuna moved slowly, its limpid blue waters inviting all to come. He dipped once, twice, three times, hands folded in prayer, a great longing in his heart. Suddenly an open booklet met his gaze. It floated right past him, and he reached out and picked it up. He read, "Jesus said, 'I am the way, the truth, and the life; no man comes to the Father but by me.'"

Who is Jesus? And where is his Father? Did he mean God? He must find this man. The *sadhu* began a new pilgrimage, this time in search of Jesus. He traveled far, always asking the same question.

"Jesus?" his companion said on the bus. "No, I don't know him. I don't think he lives around here."

"Jesus?" the travelers on the train answered. "Are you sure he lives in this part of India? We've never heard of him."

"Jesus? Jesus who?" the villager quizzed as the man stopped him on his trek from one village to the next. "Must be one of those new gurus."

But the *sadhu* kept on. Someone, somewhere, would be able to tell him where to find Jesus.

He entered Purnea Bazaar late one evening and stopped at a small tearoom to buy food. "Where is Jesus?" he asked. "I want to find Jesus."

Muni Lal, the shopkeeper, turned to some friends and exclaimed, "Govind Ram! Listen to this. The *sadhu* wants to find Jesus! Ha! Ha! Ha!" Trying to control his mirth, he said, "Jesus? Sure . . . we know all about Jesus."

"Don't mislead me, brother," the holy man pleaded. "I am serious. I want to know where he lives. I must meet him."

Govind Ram, the cloth merchant, spoke up, "You're looking for Jesus? Go to Jisu Muni. She'll tell you about him."

The owner of the tea stall handed the *sadhu* a small earthen cup filled with fresh, hot tea, and a plate of curry puffs. "My friend," he said gravely, "I apologize for laughing. I couldn't believe you meant it."

"Yes," Govind Ram added, "if you want to know about Jesus, Jisu Muni will tell you." The courthouse gong struck eleven and he continued, "But don't go now. Jisu Muni is a white lady from a foreign country. She lives in that small bungalow down the next street. You might frighten her if you disturb her now. Go in the morning."

"I'll wager she'll tell you about Jesus," Muni Lal said with a broad grin on his thin face.

"You're really sure?"

"Sure? Of course I'm sure. Why do you doubt?"

"I've searched for months, and been disappointed so often." He removed a cloth purse from his loin cloth and took out money to pay for the food.

"Put it back, friend," the shopkeeper said quietly. "It's on the house. I should pay you."

"For what?"

"We didn't realize what we have. We've scorned Jisu Muni, making fun of her zeal for Jesus. But it could be she's found the friend all of us need."

The *sadhu* turned away, new hope in his eyes. In spite of the late hour he felt he must immediately locate the house. He walked to the small bungalow, entered the compound and was challenged by a Nepali guard. "What do you want?" the watchman asked.

"Please, sir, I know it is late, but I desire to talk with Jisu Muni, the white lady from a foreign country. I am told she lives here."

"Yes," the guard replied, "but you can't see her now. Come back tomorrow morning."

"Please, sir, could I sleep here? I promise not to cause any trouble."

The Nepali searched the man's face, then grunted. "My mat is on the front verandah, where I sleep," he said. "You may spread your cloth there, too, if you wish. But you must not awaken the ladies before dawn."

"Thank you, sir. You are most kind," the *sadhu* exclaimed. He felt a sense of great expectancy. Tomorrow he would hear about Jesus.

Inside the immaculate cottage two Swiss missionaries slept, unaware that the Lord had already answered their daily prayer. Just that evening again Lilly had prayed, "Dear Lord, we're expecting you to send Elizabeth a prepared heart." They little suspected a Hindu holy man would sleep on their front verandah, waiting for dawn so that he could hear the gospel!

The first faint streaks of dawn began to tint the eastern sky when Elizabeth awakened to a call, "Jisu Muni, Jisu Muni!"

She smiled at the use of the nickname used in the bazaar, but rising, she hastily threw a robe around her and went to the door. Pushing it open slightly she peered through the crack. "Who's there?" she asked.

The *sadhu* stood before her, his lithe brown body covered sparsely with two cotton cloths, one a loin cloth, the other thrown loosely around bare shoulders. His hair, matted with cow dung, coiled on top of his head. In his hand he carried a bowl and walking stick. A small bundle and a gleaming brass vessel sat on the verandah floor. Elizabeth drew back.

"Jisu Muni," the man pleaded, "please don't leave. I have come a long journey to hear about Jesus."

"Who are you? From where do you come?" she asked, opening the door a bit wider.

He looked at her with fear-filled eyes. "Please don't leave," he reiterated. "I must hear about Jesus."

Elizabeth sensed an inner confirmation, a voice that said, "Don't fear. I have sent him."

She stepped onto the verandah and motioning to the bench said, "Friend, please wait here. I'll be with you soon." Then reentering her room she called, "Lilly, Lilly."

"What's the matter, Elizabeth? Somebody sick?"

"Lilly, get up. We have a guest for breakfast. A *sadhu* has come to hear about Jesus. I'll talk to him. He seems very determined to learn about our Lord."

"But isn't that what we expected? We asked for a prepared heart." Elizabeth could hear the smile in her friend's voice.

She chuckled, then answered, "Lilly! I never expected a Hindu holy man. I've always feared them. I must say the Lord is full of surprises."

"Yes, isn't he? But then, you'd better go and get started. I'll pray as I make breakfast."

"Thanks, Lilly. You're a brick!"

On the front verandah questions and answers flowed as the missionary and her guest began the most unusual witnessing situation in Elizabeth Liechti's twenty-year missionary career. The man said, "Jisu Muni, I've traveled all over India to rid myself of this guilt on my heart. My parents died. How can I be sure I'm forgiven for my wrongdoings against them?"

"How did you come here?"

"Never mind that," he answered earnestly. "My heart cries for peace. Please tell me about Jesus. I want to find Jesus." He drew the little booklet, much worn, out of his loin cloth. Opening to the center page he showed the words that first caught his attention. His bony finger trembled as he pointed to the words, "Jesus said, 'I am the way, the truth, and the life. No man comes to the Father, but by me.'"

Elizabeth's eyes misted. Putting aside her natural curiosity, she told again the magnificent story of God's redeeming love through Jesus, God's son.

Too soon Lilly appeared at the door, a plate of fresh potato curry and hot *chapatis* in her hands. "Friend," she said to the *sadhu*, "we've made breakfast for you."

Would he accept cooked food from Christians? Ordinarily he would consider them outcastes, but this was no ordinary moment. He looked up with the hint of tears and said, "You are too good. You shouldn't trouble yourselves for me."

"Eat, friend," Elizabeth urged. "You must be hungry from your long travels. I'll go for my breakfast while you eat here, then we'll study the Scriptures together."

The hours passed quickly as the Swiss missionary and the Hindu holy man pored over the Word of God. He kept watching the glow on her face. She radiated inner peace and joy. Could he also find it, he wondered?

The sun rose high in the heavens and its blistering heat announced another scorcher of a day. About ten o'clock Elizabeth stood up and said, "Now you must excuse me. I have to go to town."

"May I come again?" He stood with bowed head and clutched the New Testament she had given him.

"Tomorrow morning at dawn. I'll be free."

"It is good, Jisu Muni. I must meditate and read about all I have learned. I must find for myself."

Next morning the Bible study continued. Elizabeth turned to the *sadhu* and asked, "Friend, will you accept Jesus Christ as your Lord and Savior?"

He nodded.

"Will you reject all other ways?" she probed, and again he nodded his affirmation.

"Then confess your sins right now in prayer. Ask forgiveness and trust the completed work of Christ for you on the cross."

The man began to pray, and soon his heart longing and cry changed tone. A look of peace stole over his countenance. "Something has happened, brother?" Jisu Muni asked.

"Oh, Jisu Muni!" he exulted. "I didn't know it would be like this!" He drew several deep breaths, and said, "I feel so clean, so forgiven!" He joined his hands in prayer and said, "Thank you, Lord Christ! Thank you, Jisu Muni, for telling me about him."

The *sadhu* gathered his few belongings together and said, "I must go. I must return to my wife and family. They haven't seen me for five years. They probably think I'm dead, but I've come alive! Thank you, Jisu Muni! Oh, thank you!"

He walked down the lane, out the gate, and onto the busy bazaar road, but he did not go as he had come! Jisu Muni wiped a tear of joy and turned indoors. God had answered her request by sending a prepared heart.

# The case of the missing god

Bright-eyed Ajit Kumar, eight-year-old scion of the great Tiwari family, edged up to the door of their private temple and inspected the small black stone enshrined on a red velvet cushion. The idol, the size and shape of a man's thumb, bore the imposing name Mahadev (the Great God).

The boy quickly observed that for once Mahadev remained unattended. No priest? No, of course not! He and his helpers would be at the special prayers in the big house, Ajit's home. The boy figured he would remain undetected since a feast followed the religious rites. Most surely everybody would want to participate.

Ajit Kumar had eyed Mahadev for days, desiring this smooth stone for playing cowries, the Indian version of marbles. If he could play with Mahadev, he'd surely beat his best friend, Anup. Ajit was irked at his poor winning record.

With the priests and attendants absent, the boy crept into the temple. Just in case someone might be watching from the outside, he bowed before the idol. However, with the motion, he quickly swooped the stone from its cushion and dropped it into the small pocket inside the waistband of his shorts. Then he ran outside.

For the next hour or two the boys played and shouted in the streets. Ajit Kumar shot the beautiful black stone all over, and indeed, won the game. He came home flushed with victory.

The idol's disappearance caused great consternation. The head priest struck his breast and bowed low before his master.

"Your honor," he wailed, "he's gone! Something has displeased the great Mahadev. He's no longer there!"

"Nonsense!" the wealthy landlord retorted. "You've been drinking too much of my fine liquor, and you can't see straight. He must be there. I'll investigate personally."

But Ajit's father found the report to be true. Mahadev had left. "What has happened?" cried Mr. Tiwari. "What have I done to anger him?"

The priests chanted in mourning, and their master hastily arranged to consult a pundit. "Ah," the wise man said, "this is very serious . . . a great tragedy, sir. It requires large sums of money for charities, and a feast for the entire community."

"Anything! Anything!" the anguished landlord declared. He returned home to make arrangements for the appeasement of the great god, Mahadev.

In the midst of the turmoil a little boy ran to and fro. He returned from his victorious cowrie game to hear wailing. In wonder he watched the priests beating their breasts. The stone in his concealed pocket seemed to burn like fire—not literally, but just the knowledge of its being in his possession became an unbearable burden to Ajit.

But a heavy guard now watched the temple. No chance to return the idol, the boy concluded. How about the well? He ran on the pretense of getting a drink, but others were there also, and Ajit Kumar hesitated to throw Mahadev into the well in their presence. Better wait until he could find a chance to replace it on its cushion. The god hadn't harmed him yet. Another day or two would scarcely matter.

So Ajit waited until his father prepared and gave the big feast. Perhaps everyone would again leave the temple as they had done previously.

In the hustle and bustle of the feasting, a little boy ran around unnoticed. As he surmised, every guard left his post under the cover of dark to get his share of the magnificent repast at the big house. Once again Ajit tiptoed into the temple. He quickly replaced Mahadev on the red velvet cushion, then turned and ran out. But the stone's reappearance was noticed only the next day after all had slept off the results of the night's festivities.

"He's come! He's come!" they shouted. The fame of the idol spread throughout the entire area. Pilgrims now found a new site to visit. In fact, this temple became very famous.

The boy, now grown and holding a responsible government position, met a Christian missionary one night. He confessed, "I lost faith in Hinduism when I was eight years old," and recounted the above story.

The missionary asked, "Did your father ever find out what really happened? Did you tell him?"

"Not until after I earned my Master's degree," Ajit Kumar answered. "No, not until then. It took all those years for me to find enough courage to speak. But one day I asked whether he remembered the incident. How could he forget?"

"What did he say?" the missionary quizzed.

"He said he well remembered. Then I confessed I was the guilty person. I had taken Mahadev to play cowries, and in the tumult that resulted, I hid him in the concealed pocket at my waist. Padre Sahib! My father wouldn't believe me! No! He simply refused to accept my story. He said I invented it to excuse my liberal ideas learned in college, and he died without accepting my explanation."

"Is the story really true, friend?"

"Yes, Sahib Ji, on my word of honor. It broke my faith in Hinduism. I have no faith in the Hindu religion."

# The gypsy boy

The sun rose over the towns and villages on the plains of North India. Under an overspreading banyan tree on the outskirts of a small village, five-year-old Kumar awakened to find his pet monkey, Buddhu, tickling his ear.

"You rascal!" the boy exclaimed.

The little brown monkey danced up and down for joy, his red skirt bobbing in fascinating twirls. His shrieks of delight clearly meant, "Come on, it's getting late."

Kumar's parents thought so too. Ram and Sundri already had finished their breakfast. Their son quickly washed at the little stream near the tree. Kumar ate hungrily, making sure that his friend Buddhu also got some hot Indian bread and delicious potato curry. By the time they finished, Kumar's parents had packed everything in baskets which his mother lifted on her head. The gypsy family was ready to move.

Much of the trail led through flooded rice fields. Buddhu sat on Kumar's shoulder, otherwise he ran on a leash. After walking an hour the family stopped to rest by a large bamboo clump. Nearby they saw a mango tree and the boy and monkey darted over to search for ripe fruit. With a shout of triumph Kumar pulled at a low-lying branch until several mangoes fell. Buddhu grabbed one, tore the end open and began to munch. Kumar picked up two more, only to hear his father call, "Come on, it's time to move."

Ten minutes later the travelers entered the large village of Manua. "A monkey! A monkey!" the children shouted. They gathered from everywhere, shrilling, "Dance for us."

Ram unleashed the music box from his shoulder straps. As he played, Buddhu jigged and twirled to the music. The crowd cried, "More . . . more. . ." every time the monkey stopped to hold his tin out for money. The clink, clink of silver and copper coins sounded sweet to Ram and Sundri. Yes, Kumar loved this gypsy life.

However, one day everything changed.

The family entered a village where people were dying from cholera. Kumar's parents both took ill and died about sunset. Outcaste Hindus, paid for their services, came running to remove the corpses. A bewildered little boy and monkey found themselves alone.

Kumar began to cry from hunger and grief. With Buddhu beside him he searched for the people who had carried his parents away. Where had they gone? They walked up to a bazaar stall laden with food. Buddhu suddenly snatched several pieces of pastry from a plate. The man yelled, but the sobbing child said, "I'm hungry, uncle, and I've lost my parents."

"Come here, son," the man replied. He gave the boy and his companion some food before they continued their search.

Not everyone was so kind. True, some did feed the boy and his little friend, but the world soon forgot their need. Within a week Kumar and Buddhu disappeared.

Several months passed. One day Mohan Lal, a village watchman who lived some fifteen or twenty miles from Manua, decided to take the shortcut through the jungle instead of returning home by his usual route. Tall and strong, Mohan enjoyed an excellent record as guard for the village. Now, after staying awake all night, the man stretched wearily when the first streaks of dawn lit the eastern sky. He felt hungry, so he started home by a shortcut that led through thick underbrush. Suddenly he heard a strange noise.

Mohan looked up. There in a tree near the trail a scared little boy peered down from a platform shared by a large grey monkey!

"Little boy, little boy!" Mohan called. The monkey, a Lungur, bared his teeth and shook a threatening fist. The man was used to these jungle creatures and respected their strength.

What should I do, Mohan wondered. He sat on a stump far enough away to appease the monkey and watched. Finally he decided to go back and tell the chief. He's a smart man, the watchman thought. He'll make a plan to rescue the little boy.

On his return to the village he bowed low before the chief and said, "I found a little boy treed in the jungle, your honor. A big Lungur monkey is guarding him."

"What?" the man answered in amazement.

"The monkeys have captured a boy, sir," Mohan said again. "A Lungur is guarding him and he threatened when I called to the boy."

"Hmmm . . ." the man said, stroking his chin, "how big a boy?"

"Must be about four or five, sir."

"Probably the boy and monkey reported missing several months ago. I heard the parents died of cholera, but nobody knows what became of the child. But you said a Lungur?"

"Yes, sir . . . no mistaking it. "

"The dancing monkey was a Rhesus. I wonder what became of him."

"Likely chased away, your honor. He'd run for his life from a Lungur."

"True," the chief said. "Hmmm. . . ." He chewed thoughtfully on his tobacco, then spit a brown stream onto the ground before answering.

His mother came around the house and asked, "Son, what is it?"

"A likely story, Mother, one you'll scarcely believe," he replied. "Mohan Lal found a small boy treed by monkeys. We think he ought to be rescued."

"Where?"

"In the jungle between here and my home," Mohan said.

"On the trail?"

"Not the main one, ma'am, but a narrow path I take sometimes, a shortcut."

"Is the boy all right?"

"He's scared . . . and very thin."

"Poor waif," the grey-haired woman said, wiping her eyes. "Do something, Krishna."

"Of course, Mother. I'll call a village council tonight to formulate a plan. Monkeys can be dangerous, as all of us know, especially when they're guarding the boy."

That evening every member of council and many more gathered to discuss the matter. Both men and women talked loudly, arguing about the best method for outwitting the monkeys. But they finally agreed that watching came first, then rescue would follow. The men signed up in teams of two for relays around the clock.

A week . . . two weeks . . . three weeks passed. Nobody brought a good report. "Any progress?" the chief kept asking.

"No, sir," the watchmen said. "The monkeys sense we're nearby, so they're really jittery. I think they figure we're planning a rescue, so they've redoubled their efforts. In fact, sir, two of them fought over him today."

The chief's mother overheard and came onto the verandah where the chief was talking to the watchmen. "Oh," she cried, "did the monkeys hurt the little boy?"

"One cut his lip, ma'am, from above the mouth, through to his chin. I saw it bleeding."

"Oh, no, Gulta! You must rescue him, or he'll die."

"We tried, sir," the watchman told the chief.

Krishna nodded, then suggested, "Hide, and don't give up. They're feeding the boy to keep him alive, so wait until they think you've forgotten."

"Yes, your honor."

Their patience eventually paid off. Mohan and his friend Gulta hid under the bushes as usual, watching the little boy through the branches. The big Lungur monkey scanned his surroundings but saw no one. His beady black eyes darted this way and that, but eventually he decided to place a smaller monkey in charge of the hostage.

Then he uttered a call and crashed from one branch to another, his long tail securely keeping him from falling. Soon every monkey in the vicinity followed the big Lungur. Mohan and Gulta scarcely breathed, lest they disclose their hiding place. Today would be their day!

Was it a monkey picnic that lured them? We'll never know. But the small female guard soon swung down from the platform and wandered casually in the direction of the water hole. The little boy shivered in fear, alone.

"Come," Mohan whispered, "you climb, grab the boy, and toss him to me. I'll catch him and run."

Gulta went up swiftly. The boy saw him mounting and squealed, terrified. He crouched as far back as possible but big Gulta's arm grasped him, then dropped him to the ground. Mohan caught the lad, held him firmly, and ran. His companion followed quickly, sprinting hard for the edge of the jungle.

The guard monkey heard the crash, crash, crash of their flight. She looked up, darted forward and backward, then returned to the tree. Someone had stolen the boy! She swung from one tree to the next, and chased the men all the way to the edge of the jungle. One time she came so close she prepared to swoop down on them, but they reached the open fields just in time. The guard monkey shook her fist and bared her teeth, but the men and little boy were out of her reach.

Mohan and Gulta shouted their triumph. Many came out to meet them, among them, Krishna, the chief. "We can't keep him here," Krishna said. "The monkeys will raid us on their return."

"But where can we take him?" his mother asked.

"To the mission hospital, I'd say. He needs both medicine and love, and they'll give liberally. They're good people."

Everybody nodded assent, then hurried home to get their long sticks in case of assault. A large group surrounded Krishna's mother as she held the gypsy boy in her arms. The monkeys charged the men once, but they fought them off. After walking two hours the villagers reached the mission.

Little Kumar's name became Jakki, Hindi for Zacchaeus, because he had been found in a tree. Many years later the gypsy boy became a preacher and gospel singer in North Bihar. To the

end of his life he carried a nasty scar on his upper lip, and oblig-
ingly told his little friends (of which the author was one) the story
of his rescue from the monkeys. Jakki would conclude by saying,
"That's the way the Lord Jesus took care of me, to keep me alive
so that I might preach the gospel."

*After these things I looked, and behold, a great multitude which no one could number, of all nations, tribes, peoples, and tongues, standing before the throne and before the Lamb, clothed with white robes, with palm branches in their hands, and crying out with a loud voice, saying, "Salvation belongs to our God who sits on the throne, and to the Lamb!"*

*All the angels stood around the throne and the elders and the four living creatures, and fell on their faces before the throne and worshiped God, saying:*

*"Amen! Blessing and glory and wisdom,*
*Thanksgiving and honor and power and might,*
*Be to our God forever and ever.*
*Amen."*

Revelation 7:9-12
New King James Version

# The
# Conqueror

*The road to Howrah Bridge, Calcutta*

# Road to Howrah Bridge

On a busy wintry afternoon in Calcutta, India, a wandering sacred bull butted a too-curious foreign tourist who dared push him aside at the approach to the city's famed Howrah Bridge. A traffic policeman looked, and grinned. Cyclists, tinkling their bells, laughed outright, as did crowds of pedestrians. Among them stood Roger Simms, an Anglo-Indian orphan, aged fourteen. Dressed in faded jeans, blue knit shirt and lightweight coat, all laboriously hand-washed, he stopped on the opposite street corner, his favorite entertainment spot. He placed his modest lunch pail and thermos on a low wall and perched himself to get a good view.

The tourist recovered his hat and sunglasses after the bull's surprise attack. Roger's brown eyes filled with mirth as his drawn features relaxed into a rare smile. He watched the Americans board a streetcar, heard the clanging of the bell as it carried them and hundreds of commuters to Tolleygunj. The policeman turned back to daily pressures of directing traffic, and the boy drew a deep breath as he jumped down. Taking his lunch pail and thermos, he turned homeward, feet dragging and shoulders slumped.

Howrah Bridge made Roger's life bearable. The silvery sheen of India's famous cantilever bridge served as foreground to the slow-moving Hooghly River that separated Calcutta from its suburb, Howrah. Roger daily anticipated this interlude, watching the flurry and flow of masses thronging the railway station opposite. It came sandwiched between dreary hours at the garment factory and Adrian Clont's pressures at home, if their attic room could be called a home.

In their cramped quarters under the eaves of a downtown apartment building the boys sweltered in summer and chilled in winter. Six months earlier the Catholic orphanage had moved Adrian and Roger into this accommodation, designating the eighteen-year-old as guardian to the younger. Initially it seemed an acceptable arrangement—until Adrian changed. Roger frowned. Confound those despicable drugs and the lure of easy money!

To escape meeting his roommate, Roger retired early, and rose before dawn. Not until the factory bell announced the close of another workday did the boys meet.

Adrian awaited Roger outside the factory's main gate. Of stocky build and swarthy complexion, he looked older than his years. Now he glanced at the tall youth. With eyes glinting slyly, like a cat watching its prey, Adrian said softly, "Last chance, babe! Want to make an easy haul with me tonight? You could use an extra hundred, couldn't you?"

Roger tensed, then blurted out, "No way . . . not on your life!"

"Mama's clean, clean boy!"

The handsome youth shot his companion a piercing glance that resulted in Adrian's foulest language, to be followed by, "Keep your mouth shut . . . or else!" With a shrug the older lad slipped into the waiting crowds to become an unknown among thousands of homegoing workers. Roger, still smarting from the unwelcome encounter, winced. Hunching forward as he faced the biting wind on that wintry afternoon, he, too, became one among many in India's largest city.

How long could he resist Adrian's pressures? Today's blatant threats meant that his roommate's white-hot temper would sure-ly lash out against him, especially if Adrian returned half drunk as usual. Roger shuddered, and his shoulders sagged. Utterly dejected he walked toward Howrah Bridge. Would to God he had a confidante, someone with whom to share!

One of the greatest cities in the world throbbed around him. Until Adrian began haunting his life six weeks back, the move-ment and thrill of Calcutta captivated Roger, but not now. The throaty cries of a straggling band of marchers rose over the din of clanging cycle bells and creaking streetcars. They strung along the crowded sidewalk, in the street, a voice of protest in a city where millions believe that fate decrees both time and circumstance. Six weeks earlier Roger would have joined them, just for the sheer exuberance of sharing something alive. But again, that was before Adrian changed, and sought to involve his room companion.

Factories now gave way to rows of individual houses, smaller initially and identical in their boxlike concrete structures. Farther on, however, older homes bordered the street, some with compounds marked by five-foot brick walls to ensure privacy. Clinging ivy vines gave one spacious bungalow the sense of something lasting, a house that had stood perhaps for a hundred years. Roger liked it best.

A wooden structure with overhanging eaves and box windows filled with red geraniums and sweet-faced pansies, it reminded the lonely boy of the small apartment he and Mums shared in another such building some eight hundred miles south of Calcutta. But all that had changed six years ago when his beautiful mother dropped on the schoolroom floor one day. Her son, sole survivor, was sent to relatives in this big city. Life might have been different if Uncle Len hadn't refused to keep him. Roger drew a deep breath, then thought . . . what's the use? Uncle Len, the orphanage, Adrian. . . . He wiped a quick tear.

But the house continued to draw him back. He purposely walked this route to the factory so he could pass it, and often he'd stop at the gate to remember Mums and the parties they hosted on sunny afternoons. Sometimes this wide verandah also resounded with laughter as a bevy of well-dressed young people milled around an older woman with a beautiful smile. She seemed a queen among them, her plain features transformed by love.

One morning he saw the lady in her garden. She looked up from cutting roses and waved, a gesture which he shyly returned. It became something of a ritual, with the lonely boy often standing at the gate wondering whether he would catch a glimpse of his friend. Those cheerful salutes became cherished treasures for him to reexamine when life seemed unbearable.

Today, however, the big house sat silent. The empty verandah and drawn curtains shouted that this meager joy, like all others, had evaporated with time. Tears surfaced as Roger rushed on, seeking to put the house behind him. Nobody cared! Nobody!

A steady flow of traffic rumbled past, with the tinkling of bells as rickshaws wove in and out of the crush that characterizes Calcutta's streets. Roger barely noticed Howrah Bridge today. He wanted privacy, refuge. Ten minutes later he approached the decrepit apartment building in which he lived.

Several children clustered around a peanut vendor outside. A leaking pipe formed a puddle of water at the curbside, and two barefoot children gaily paddled in it despite the cold wind. They laughed at Roger and waved as he began ascending steps—up, up, up to the very top.

He stopped before the door to the attic room and took his key, hung on a string around his neck. Entering, he carefully fastened the latch, then knelt before his wooden cot. With another key hung on the same string he opened a tin trunk hidden under the bed. Roger's hands shook as he clasped two pictures—one of his parents on their wedding day; the other an enlargement of his father, a handsome naval officer who died in a storm at sea when Roger was less than a year old.

"Oh, God . . . oh, God!" The boy sobbed. "Please tell me what to do. I can't stay here! I hate this room. I want to go home. . . . I want parents to love me!"

The putrid stale air pressed in as he clutched his precious pictures. Outside he heard the raucous cawing of the crows and the roar from the city streets, but he remained on his knees until a little mouse scurried across his shoe. Rising hastily, Roger replaced the pictures, carefully locked the trunk, and turned to leave. God had not spoken. Only Howrah Bridge remained. He closed his eyes, imagining the soothing waters of the Hooghly River flowing over his head. Yes, they would welcome him as a mother welcomes her child.

Out on the street he pulled his thin coat closer and tried to blot out hunger pangs, easily allayed by the two *rupees* in his pocket. Instead he hastened, drawn irresistibly, weaving in and out of traffic. When he approached the bridge, he skidded down the bank to hide under the great girders. Now, away from everyone, with darkness to hide him, he could assess the best place to jump.

But the blazing lights from Howrah Railway Station on the opposite banks of the river arrested his attention. A shrill train whistle flashed a thousand memories. The boy wiped a tear, then noted little lights from shanties beyond the station. There, behind mud walls, parents and children were sitting down to eat their evening meals. Roger began to sob.

"I don't want to die, God! I want to live! Oh, God, aren't you listening?" Someone seemed to touch him on the shoulder. He looked up, amazed. "Is it you, God? Oh . . . I hope so. Please . . . I want parents . . . a home . . . please!"

Calmly he turned back to the street and along his usual route to work. "God," he said, "where are you leading me? The lady with the beautiful smile isn't home. The house was dark."

Nevertheless, he tried the gate, relieved to find it would open. He walked up the path between rosebushes bearing red blooms. Their sweet fragrance reached him with promise. Could God bring something beautiful out of his thorny past?

Roger climbed the four steps onto the verandah lined with potted plants and made his way to the front door. Only when he knocked did he feel a moment of panic. What if someone came?

The door opened slightly, and the lady with the beautiful smile stood there. She switched on the light, looked through a crack and saw the boy. "Ma'am, I've come," he said.

Rosie Paul threw the door open. "You've come? Come to see me? Oh, I'm glad! Look, your hands are blue with cold, and your coat's thin."

She drew him to the warm kitchen where he saw a table set for two. Where were the young people?

"Now tell me about yourself," she began after they sat on each side of a blazing fire. "I don't even know your name."

"Roger Simms."

"Your parents?"

He shook his head. "No, ma'am, not for the last six years. Dad died at sea. He was First Mate on the S.S. *Karim*."

She nodded, her eyes intent on his face, then asked, "Your mother?"

"You remind me of her, ma'am, especially when you smile." Roger shifted uneasily, then continued, "Mom taught in the Nizam's school in Hyderabad. We lived in an apartment of a big house something like this one." After a moment's silence he added, "One day she died of a heart attack, when I was eight. They sent me to my relatives here in Calcutta, but Uncle Len wouldn't keep me." He drew a deep breath as his brown eyes glistened with tears. He bowed his head, struggling to regain composure.

The story continued falteringly. Rosie's intimate knowledge of city ways warned her he might be lying, but an inner voice assured her he needed help. What would Jack say?

Ten minutes later her husband, Brigadier Paul, entered with arms filled with groceries. He plunked the bags onto a counter and asked, "Rosie, what's happened to Ram? I can never depend on that boy! He should have been out there to help me carry these in." Then he glanced at the stranger who had jumped to his feet and said, "Oh? We have a guest?"

"Yes, Jack," she answered with a smile, "a friend of mine, Roger Simms. We've seen each other often, but this is my first chance to really talk. He's orphaned . . . and needs a home. As for Ram . . . well, his mother sent for him early to attend an uncle's funeral, and you know what that means. He may be gone a week!"

"Huh!" the man grunted while his wife worked as she talked, setting the table for three and filling the glasses with water. Roger drew a deep breath, his hands clutched until his knuckles looked white under the tan. He hoped he wouldn't be thrown out.

Brigadier Paul carefully removed his misted glasses, wiped them, then replaced them before saying, "Come here, my boy. Roger, is it? Don't be afraid."

The tall lad managed the two yards between them to stand before Rosie's husband. Jack placed his hands on the boy's shoulders and searched his face. Looking deep into those anxious brown eyes he said softly, "You're orphaned and looking for a home? We're without children, longing for a son. Want to try?"

"But . . . but . . . the young people, sir. I've seen them. . . ."

Rosie laughed, and said, "He's seen the tribe, Jack . . . out on the verandah."

Jack Paul's eyes twinkled as he said, "The tribe? They're our nieces and nephews. They descend upon us at times to pick their uncle and aunt's pockets! Come, son, let's eat, and I'll hear your story after we get some of Mom's delicious stew. I'm starved . . . and I'll wager you are too."

# Why God scattered the team

Seated at my desk in the Audience Relations Department of Far East Broadcasting's India headquarters, I, Leoda Buckwalter, checked my figures. There it was again—East Godavari District in Andhra Pradesh kept coming through with consistently high numbers of letters from listeners in this southern state. The Telugu programs beamed over FEBA Seychelles were doing their work! Moreover, an outstanding percentage came from Hindus, asking for Bible Correspondence Courses! We began to see supernatural design and purpose at work, and with the rest of our FEBA Staff in Bangalore we prayed earnestly for East Godavari District.

Therefore we took alarm when the entire radio staff of these Telugu programs was suddenly terminated by their church council. True, others replaced them, but all were novices. Why would God allow this to happen? Therein lies our story.

It began with two major factions seeking supremacy within the newly formed state. The Teleganas populated the inland areas around Hyderabad, their capital, and the former home of the fabulously wealthy Nizam, sometimes quoted as the wealthiest man in the world. Yet his subjects knew little of the advancement enjoyed by the Andhras, those Telugu-speaking peoples who resided in the coastal plains administered by the British. Understandably, the Andhras learned skills that earned them prestigious seats in industry, business, and even government when the Royal State of the Nizam joined the Republic of India in 1947. Jealousy soon erupted.

In a land fragmented by language and cultural differences, riots make stale reading, but we noted with alarm the intensity of the Telegana-Andhra dispute. Then came the stunning news that the entire Andhra staff of this particular set of Christian radio programs had been terminated by a church who wanted only Teleganas in power, not Andhras! Political tensions had seeped into the church and taken their course.

From Anne Ediger, the missionary who trained the team and supervised the radio work, on down to the last member, all were brokenhearted. Anne, our friend, used her expertise to the end of her days in training nationals to do the work she knew so well. Her assignments took her first to Manila, to work with FEBC Radio International, then brought her back to India to work with FEBA India, Back to the Bible, and the Evangelical World Fellowship. Through her we learned the sequel of a team that suddenly found itself disrupted and scattered. Some sought higher training in the West, others found other employment, but one man, E.Y. Samuel, walked into high adventure when he left his office. We presume to follow him in what must have been something like this:

Samuel, a slightly-built man with a bit of a stoop from sitting long years at a desk, cleared his work for the last time. Conflict raged, but almost through tears the man said, "I don't understand, God! But I know that you know more than I do . . . so I accept."

He checked notebooks and files. Replacing them, his hand fell on lists from East Godavari District. Thoughts flashed . . . Samuel! Remember East Godavari District? All those Hindus . . . all those completed Bible Correspondence Courses? Ah!

He pushed his hair back from his eyes, took up the book and began to study it thoughtfully. "Hmmm . . . " he murmured, "looks like well over 1,500 names and addresses here. And where do I find certificates bearing my signature? On the wall of a hut, or perhaps in the office of a lawyer, doctor, or professor. Samuel," he addressed himself with a smile, "you have more need of this than anyone else. Get busy, man! God knows what he's doing!"

He tucked the list into his briefcase, cleared his desk, turned off the light and closed the door for the last time. His determined step and the new light in his eyes anticipated high adventure ahead, not defeat.

Making arrangements at home to leave for awhile, the man journeyed to East Godavari District. He began knocking on doors. He tried the first house, not sure of his reception.

"Who's there?" a male voice called.

"Your brother, E.Y. Samuel."

A tall man looked out from the slightly opened door. "I don't believe I know you," he said.

"Oh, yes," his guest answered. "I wrote you letters when you sent in your lessons for the Bible Correspondence Course, and I signed your certificate. I represent the radio work."

The door opened a bit more. Rolla Ram answered, "Radio? Yes, brother? Your name again?"

"E.Y. Samuel."

He waited while the man walked over to check the certificate hanging on the wall. Rolla Ram rushed back and opened the door wide, saying, "Yes, yes, it is the same! See here? It's your name on my certificate!"

Samuel drew a deep breath and sent an arrow prayer to heaven. Thank you, Lord. Now open his heart. He said aloud, "Have you pencil and paper? Let me sign my name, and you can compare the signatures."

"The same!" Rolla Ram's expansive gesture spoke volumes as he invited his guest to enter this simple mud hut with tile roof that sat in a village of modest size, midst cultivated fields.

A wooden cot sat in one corner, and grain bins lined the walls. In another corner a woman stir-fried vegetables in an iron vessel. She looked up as she squatted before the humble stove, pulled her *saree* more firmly over her head as she worked, but smiled.

Chickens roosted near the grain bins. Two small children had already fallen asleep on a mat. A kerosene lamp glowed from the table by the bed. Rolla Ram pulled out a wooden chair and offered it to his guest. Samuel thanked him and sat while Rolla Ram stood nearby, rubbing his hands together in great pleasure.

Samuel's quick glance located pictures of Hindu gods and goddesses high on one wall, but under them, recessed into a shelf by itself, stood the radio. More important, beside the radio was a Telugu Bible.

Rolla Ram was speaking, "Sir, we are regular listeners to your programs, and we never miss a day in reading the Bible. Perhaps you will read it for us tonight? And you must stay with us. We are honored to have you come."

Samuel looked around, noting a lean-to outside. "Please don't concern yourself about me," he said. "I can sleep anywhere. I've brought my things with me. All I need is a mat."

"Oh, no, my brother. God has sent you to our humble home. You are blessing us with your presence and teaching. We want to hear more about the Lord Jesus and his way of salvation."

Quality time, thought Samuel. Prepared hearts! What more could anyone ask?

Not only did Rolla Ram and his family accept Jesus Christ as Savior and Lord, but they took down the Hindu pictures and asked for baptism. Then they made their home a center for Christian worship and outreach to their community.

Samuel had never known such results in all his years of ministry. His high adventure took him from one home to the next with the same openhearted acceptance. New believers formed into fellowships, with this former office worker organizing them into churches. He couldn't keep up with the demands, so he quickly called for a former team member, R.K. Murthy, speaker on the radio programs. Together they established forty-five churches! The circle completed when the new churches became accepted members of the wider fellowship that had previously terminated E.Y. Samuel and R.K. Murthy because they were Andhras!

How did all this happen? Was it just E.Y. Samuel or R.K. Murthy's doings? Did the chance wind of circumstance blow, or was there a planned purpose behind every detail? We prefer to believe the latter.

The Bible Society of India began the chain of events when their representatives distributed Bibles widely in East Godavari District at highly subsidized rates. Hindus bought profusely. Ten years of effective radio programming in Telugu followed with the speaker, R.K. Murthy, offering the Bible Correspondence Courses to all who requested materials.

However, even as the seed was being sown and nurtured, harvest was ripening—but no reaping would occur while Samuel and Murthy continued working in the well-trained group. God had to scatter the team, to get his key personnel out of the office and studio and onto the road, knocking on doors. He used politics entering the church to do his work!

Anne Ediger and we reflected that had either Samuel or his preacher friend turned bitter in spirit, the whole purpose of the Lord of the Harvest would have been thwarted. History records that by the grace of God they allowed termination of the work they loved to be turned into a new door of opportunity. So the miracle of grace continued.

The last we heard, R.K. Murthy continues to speak to his people over the air, and no doubt the number of new churches thus established far exceeds our latest reports. But to all of us in FEBA India, the loveliest part of this story was the inclusion of the new fellowships into the older, established churches. Isn't that characteristic of our God's workings? He completes the circle!

# The forbidden room

There it was again, this sinister feeling of evil she couldn't understand. Mary, a beautiful South Indian bride of sixteen who lived with her husband's parents, heard an insistent voice, "Marykutty! Marykutty! Where are you?"

The open-faced Malayalee girl ran in from the garden and said, "Oh, Papa, I'm sorry. I was working outside."

The elderly gentleman with greying hair and piercing black eyes smiled slightly, then said, "No matter, girl, but I do need this immediately." He pressed a piece of paper into her hand and she noted what looked like a recipe.

"Bring it to me in the front room at the right, but remember, you're not allowed in there. Just knock. I'll open the door and take the mixture."

"Yes, Papa."

The girl recoiled at the finished product. She had but mixed spices together, yet it looked like blood! Covering the dish with a white cloth, she carried it to the forbidden room and knocked. The door opened a crack. Her father-in-law's hand reached out for the mixture, then quickly closed the door.

The girl again felt that sinister evil presence. She shuddered, and a flush of anger caused stinging tears. What was her George doing in there? What compulsion threatened their marriage? She determined to find out.

Bride and groom had barely returned from their honeymoon at Kovakulam Beach in Trivandrum when this trouble started. He was withholding something from her.

They seemed eminently suited to each other, a match arranged by their parents. George commanded respect with his athletic build and good looks, not to mention his college degree. Mary came from a wealthy Christian family, known for charitable enterprises. Both families belonged to the Syrian Orthodox Church, known locally as Jacobites. Mary anticipated regular church attendance, as was her habit, but found her husband's family negligent in this respect.

Mary had tried to talk about the forbidden room before. Now she approached George again, asking, "George, what does Papa do with the mixture I make?"

He touched her lightly on the cheek, then answered abruptly, "Darling, there are some things I don't talk about. That's one. Never ask me again, and don't you dare ask anybody else. Understand?"

She nodded numbly, trying to keep her composure. Her husband turned and walked out the door; the girl fell to her knees.

"Oh, God," she whispered, "something's terribly wrong. I don't know what it is, but I'm part of something I don't understand. Please, Lord, show me." Tears coursed down her cheeks as she continued praying. Finally she arose with a new sense of direction.

Mary began to study the people who used the forbidden room. They came at all hours of the day or night. Her father-in-law kept no regular work hours, no nine to five routine. Furthermore, his patients, if such they were, all seemed fearful, furtive. Mary heard no conversation, no pleasantries with the rest of the family—just that silent, demanding quest. For what? She shivered in fear.

Time and again the girl prayed until her peace was restored, especially after giving the prescribed mixture to her father-in-law.

Then came the day when a calmness stole over her spirit and an inner voice said, "Mary, my child, they're performing witchcraft in that room. I've placed you here to stop it."

The girl cried out softly, "Lord! Can it be? You mean my father-in-law is a wizard, a witch doctor? And he's teaching my George his craft? No, no, Lord! I can't stand it." Hot tears flowed as she continued, "Forgive me, my God, for being part of this terrible sin. My parents didn't know, nor did I, but now I've married George. What shall I do?"

"What you're doing now," the small inner voice directed. "You can pray. I do mighty things through prayer."

That began her vigil against the witchcraft that controlled the home. Each time the secret rites proceeded in the forbidden room, George's young wife fought in prayer for her husband's preservation.

She found an unexpected ally, her radio. The Malayalam Bible readings brought the Word of God into her home and encouraged her in this daily battle against evil. She fought not only for her husband, but now for the two sons the Lord gave. They must never turn to witchcraft.

One day the lads tried to follow their father into the forbidden room. "Come, boys," Mary called.

"But we want to go, too. Why can't we be with Daddy?"

"He has work to do with Grandpa," she explained. "You stay with me. Would you like to listen to the radio?"

Mary increased her vigilance in prayer. She also took the boys to church, but they found the lengthy Syriac liturgy boring and asked, "Why does the priest chant in another language, Ma?"

"That's Syriac," she answered, "the language our churches have used ever since the Apostle Thomas came to India. You remember I told you about him?"

The boys nodded, then John complained, "We can't understand, and Ma, why can't we run around like the other boys?"

Mary hugged the boy and said, "I know it's difficult, but you must remember you're in God's house, and you must reverence him." She looked at the clock, then continued, "Come, it's almost time for our favorite radio program. Now you can hear God's Word in your own mother tongue. See? That's much better, isn't it?"

One memorable day George said, "Darling, I simply don't understand."

Mary looked up and asked, "What?"

"I was an honor student in college, but regardless of all my efforts, my father's giving me up as a lost cause. I simply can't grasp the secrets of his craft."

"Oh?"

He nodded, then added, "I'll have to go to farming. I don't see any alternative."

Her eyes shone as she exclaimed, "But George, farming's an honorable way of life. You'll do well. I know you will."

George settled the family on a farm about a mile from his parents. At last Mary was free from contact with the forbidden room.

But there's more to the story. One day the boys noticed a motor car coming in the driveway. In excitement they alerted their mother, "Ma! Somebody's coming. We have guests!"

An American couple and a tall, Malayalee gentleman came up the walk. K.C. Mammen spoke to the mother and sons. His cultured, soft voice said, "I'm your nephew, K.C. Mammen, Aunt Mary, and these are my friends, Mr. and Mrs. Scott."

The woman looked surprised, then invited them in. "K.C. Mammen?" she said wonderingly. "I haven't seen you in years, not since you went to the Gulf to work. Yet your voice seems familiar."

"I'm in Bangalore now," he added, as his aunt and cousins grasped his hands and drew him into the kitchen.

"Bangalore!" she shouted, laughing. "Bangalore! You're doing the 'Malayalam Bible Readings'? Mammen!"

"Yes, Aunt Mary. I've been doing the 'Malayalam Bible Readings' for the past number of years."

So Mary's nephew had helped her battle against witchcraft. The family cleaned out the forbidden room when George's father died. The door stayed open. Moreover, one of George's sons became a preacher of the gospel. Mary won on an extremely tough assignment.

*"Sister Anne" (right) with the author at a women's meeting*

# Vow of gratitude

## *David's vow*

David Dharmaraj, esteemed headmaster of the local village school in Kattapuram, South India, wiped his brow as he parked his bicycle on the front verandah of his home. The sun's rays already penetrated the thick foliage of the jackfruit tree in the front yard. David frowned as he noted he was fifteen minutes later than usual in returning from early morning Mass. But then, how could he refuse the priest's request to advise him on a sticky problem?

He had pedalled home faster than usual. The headmaster dared not be late for opening lest his staff get the idea that time doesn't matter.

Upon entering the house David found Benji and Anne playing marbles on the living room floor. "Get up, Benji!" he yelled. "Did you bring in the eggs?"

"Yes, Papa, six this morning," his eleven-year-old replied.

"Well, change your shirt, lazy creature! Why aren't you ready for school? You have to leave in ten minutes."

"Yes, Papa." The boy disappeared into a back bedroom used by the three brothers.

"Come, pet." David scooped his six-year-old onto his lap and tweaked her chubby cheek. "You'll be a good girl today, won't you, Anne?"

"Please, Papa, why can't I go to school with the boys? I'm learning from Benji, you know."

"You what?"

She smiled and repeated, "Benji is teaching me each evening."

The man muttered, "Impossible! All right, Anne, Benji can do some of my chores tonight, and in his place I'll teach you. You'd like that, wouldn't you?"

She drew back, then said in a small voice, "Yes, Papa . . . but can't I go to school?"

"Not in this town where girls have no place in the educational system," he muttered angrily. "Now run along, pet, and we'll begin your training tonight."

Striding into the kitchen he noted his wife struggling with knots in Mary's hair as the nine-year-old cried in protest. Her father's black eyes blazed. "Mary!" he yelled. "Stop that noise! Sheela, what is this? Where's my breakfast? Don't you know I have to leave in fifteen minutes?"

His wife laid the brush on the counter and said, "Mary, do it yourself. Papa has come." Turning quietly, she said, "Your potato curry and *dosa* are ready. Come, sit down."

The thin little woman, hastily dressed in a grey housecoat over her floor-length petticoat, sighed. She took the steaming curry from the aluminum kettle, placed it on the wafer thin, eight-inched, pancake-like *dosa* she had made out of rice flour. Bringing it to her husband she asked, "Have a good ride today, David? I was worried when you came in fifteen minutes late."

"Be still, woman! No time to talk." He devoured his food, washing it down with the hot coffee Sheela brought. Then without further word, he turned and dashed for his bicycle.

It's always the same, Sheela thought sadly. No time for any of us . . . except Anne. Thank God he does take notice of her.

Indeed, tutoring his youngest provided David his highest joy. Her mental acumen, happy chatter, and aptitude for science, arts, and language challenged him to give his best. She grew into a likeable young girl, then a willowy teenager.

Anne, newly turned sixteen, caught cold at the long marriage festivities of her elder sister, Mary. It turned into flu, then pneumonia threatened. David frantically sought medical help, prayed long, fervent prayers at the cathedral, and saw his daughter recover. But instead of the joyous outgoing girl he had known, he now came home each day to wan smiles, her almost nonexistent appetite, and glass bangles far too large for his favorite daughter's fragile wrists.

All the boys now lived away from home—two married, and Benji in college in Madras. Mary's wedding now left only Anne with her parents. One day, after two months of seeing his daughter languishing, David Dharmaraj's wrath boiled over. It happened at the dinner table as he and Anne ate together. Her mother hovered in the background, serving their needs.

Anne, as usual, toyed with her meal. Her father watched her intently then commanded, "That's enough playing. Now eat your food!"

"Yes, Papa." The girl rolled some rice and curry into a small ball with her fingers, flipped it into her mouth and swallowed it. A look of anguish covered her face.

"What's the matter, pet?"

"Sorry, Papa, I feel like vomiting." The girl rose hastily, rushed to the sink, and gave up what little she had eaten.

"She's been this way for the past two weeks," Sheela said. "I took her to the doctor again yesterday, but he keeps saying there's nothing basically wrong with her. I don't know what more we can do."

David pushed his chair back. Eyes blazing, he shouted, "Well, I know what to do! Get her best dress out, Sheela. She's going with me to the cathedral in half-an-hour."

"What for, Papa?" Tears trickled down Anne's wan cheeks as she whispered in alarm.

"Anne, I'm placing you before the altar! I'm going to leave you there until God heals you. The priest will anoint you with oil like he does the others who come each day."

"Must we, Papa? I'd rather sleep. Oh, my head. . . ."

Her father stood and pounded his fist and shouted, "I tell you, I'm finished with this apathy! I can't stand this. You used to be so lively, so interested in everything. Mother, get her best dress, and don't expect us back until she's healed!"

A half-hour later a hired oxcart stopped at the door. David lifted his daughter in his arms and settled her amidst the straw, then jumped onto the front to sit with the driver. As the oxen jogged along slowly at the incredible pace of three miles an hour the man said again, "Anne, you understand me, don't you? I'm leaving you at the altar until God touches you. We've come for healing!"

She whispered, "Yes, Papa," then sank back against the pillows her mother had placed under her head. The wearisome hour-and-a-half journey brought them to the church. David picked his daughter up, carried her into the sanctuary and placed her in a heap before the altar. Others came and went; the girl remained.

"She may go now," Father Luke remarked after he had anointed and prayed for her.

"Oh, no, Father," his parishioner replied, "not until heaven hears, and the girl is healed. We're not moving from this altar. Please carry on with your business, but leave us to place our petition before God." Anne almost fainted from those strenuous hours of waiting and pleading.

Suddenly she felt an inner fire go through her being, from head to foot. God had heard! She jumped to her feet and shouted, "I'm healed, Papa, I'm healed! God did it!"

Father and daughter knelt together in wonder. Hands uplifted, David Dharmaraj said, "Lord God of heaven and earth, you have heard my feeble prayers and given my daughter back to me. Now I present her to you for your purposes, to live for you alone."

In answer to that vow Anne entered the convent to live a life of poverty and service as a Roman Catholic nun. Her proud parents followed her progress eagerly. On the day when she took her final vows of renunciation, her father said, "Anne, you belong to God. Serve him and the church."

The vibrant young nun smiled and replied, "Thank you, Papa, for insisting we stay at the altar until something happened. God heard our prayers."

Her parents continued following the girl through her seven years of preparation in France, then five more in Australia. David wrote long letters, and looked for Anne's in return. He felt her accomplishments in public health services and promotional work to be an extension of his own efforts to educate her. When Sister Anne returned to India, this Tamilian nun now knew seven languages!

But sixteen years of life in an Indian convent stifled the nun who had lived so long abroad. She met steady opposition in a land where women's paths are clearly defined—get married, serve your husband and family; live within the shadow of your family circle.

David hadn't heard from his daughter for several months, and her silence troubled him. He knew her to be strong-willed, as was he. But then, perhaps she possessed other strengths that would help mute any problems. He waited for word.

One evening as the man sat on the front verandah reading the *Evening News* he looked down the tree-lined road that fronted his home and gasped. A lone figure in white trudged the dusty trail, suitcase in hand. Could it be Anne? It looked her shape, but where was her nun's habit? Good God! Anne in a *saree*? No!

The man stood, shaded his eyes to take away the sun's glinting glare and sought to will that figure to be someone other than his daughter. "No, my God!" he said. "It can't be Anne! I won't allow it to be Anne!" He sat back exhausted, his hands shaking as he gripped the arms of the wicker chair and waited.

"Papa, Papa! I've come," she called joyously. "Oh, I'm longing to see you. So much has happened."

He said nothing. Wrath, cold and biting, rose within. He froze, awaiting her approach. Then, scathingly he said, "You've come here? Looking like this? Why?"

"I've been ill, Papa, and the doctor says I can't take institutional life any more. I have to do my own cooking he says, but I'm still working for the church and doing social work."

"You left the convent?"

The nun faltered slightly. Placing her suitcase on the ground, she extended a pleading hand and began to come up the steps.

"Stop! Answer my question!"

"Yes, Papa, I left the convent on doctor's advice."

His face set as ice. "I don't care on whose advice you left the convent, woman. I gave you to God!" His voice rose, thin and cutting, "You've renounced that vow? No! Never!"

"No, Papa, I haven't renounced any vows. I still belong to God and I'm serving him and the church."

"As long as you're out of the convent you're no daughter of mine. Don't call me Papa. You're a sinner! You have turned your back on God."

Anne stepped back, aghast. "You can't mean that, Papa. I thought you loved me."

"I loved the girl God healed," he muttered, looking beyond her to the dusty road and fields. "I loved the one who gave herself to be a nun. I don't know you. You aren't my daughter. Go!"

She shifted uneasily, trying to break this barrier, this bad dream, and replied, "Go? But I haven't seen Mama yet."

"She isn't your mother," the man spit out. "You have forfeited our love and your place at our table. You are a sinner because you broke your vow."

A tear trickled down her cheek. She reached up to wipe it away, but another followed, and another. "Please, Papa, please listen. I didn't break any vows. I'm still serving God. The only difference is that I'll live in my own apartment and do my own cooking. I'm still working for the church." She waited mutely, her lips quivering.

His voice cut the stillness. "Quit your blubbering, girl. I tell you, I don't know you! I don't know where you live or who you are. My daughter stays in the convent and performs her vows to God."

David Dharmaraj stood up, walked to the door and opened it. He heard the woman pleading, "Papa, please . . . " but with unflinching gaze he disappeared inside what had been her home. The thud of the closed door padlocked the separation between father and daughter.

The man sat down to weep, but no tear came. His heart seemed to have turned to stone. His dream had shattered, and Anne was no more.

# *Benji's gift*

Sister Anne turned slowly, retracing her steps to the town she had left an hour before. Busses honked their approach and oxcarts, now filled with women and children, veered to let them pass. Cyclists and pedestrians hurried home from market, some carrying produce in baskets on their heads. Anne tried not to see them. She trudged on, a forlorn woman, her steps weighted by the load in her heart, her mind numbed by the finality of rejection.

No renunciation vows had affected the vast sense of loneliness now engulfing the nun. For forty-eight years Anne's life revolved around a strong father figure. His proud letters filled with admonition supported her during testing times. Now David Dharmaraj had turned his back on her.

"You are a sinner! You have broken your vows!" The words kept ringing during that long evening as she approached other members of her family. But her two brothers and elder sister had already received a phone call informing them of her presence and status. None dared give her refuge. Even though Mary asked forgiveness with tears for turning her away, she too feared her father's terrible wrath. The disheartened nun spent the night at the railway station, then took the morning train for Madras where she rested and cleaned up prior to boarding the bus for the Railway Hospital Colony where Benji lived.

Would he listen? She hadn't seen him in years. Perhaps he had changed. Her steps dragged as she approached the small quarters provided for hospital staff. Could Benji help her get a hold on things? Life lay in shambles.

Anne knocked, and her brother opened the door. His round face wreathed in smiles as he exclaimed, "Come in! Come in! Suzy, it's Anne!" The nun drew a deep breath, stepped inside and placed her suitcase by the door. Her quick perusal took in a room, about twelve feet wide and fourteen feet long, mats spread on the floor, a small coffee table on one side, a divan on the other. Three boys aged about five to twelve looked up from their books. Perhaps Benji had been tutoring them.

Two teenaged girls hurried in from the back verandah with Benji's beautiful wife in tow. Everyone talked at once. "Anne!"

"Auntie! Is it really you?"

"Oh, you're so nice . . . let me hug you!"

Acceptance almost smothered the half-stunned woman standing there, wondering if this was true.

Suzy took charge. "Girls, bring ice cream. We must celebrate. Boys, go out and play. Anne, you and Benji can talk on the front verandah, and I'll finish dinner." Amid laughter the room soon emptied.

Seated in two wicker chairs Anne and Benji reminisced, but first they had to fill in background. She breathed deeply. In front she saw a neatly kept yard filled with phlox, begonias, and a gardenia bush. "Always did like gardening," Benji said with a chuckle. "With the house overflowing, we tend to get in each other's way, so I spend my evenings out here after tutoring the boys. Now Anne," he said, turning full attention on his sister, "what brings you to our humble home? I'm delighted."

"Bless you, Benji," she said, wiping a tear. "You're the first one in the family to speak kindly to me, since I left the convent, that is."

He looked at her quickly. "You've been home?"

She nodded, and he queried further, "You've left the convent? Dad saw you dressed in a *saree* instead of a nun's habit?"

Another nod while she wiped tears.

"Well, you don't need to tell me! I understand. Hmmm . . . so you've had a bad time of it." He touched her lightly on the shoulder and added, "I'm glad you came. We don't have much to offer, but we can manage until we get you safely settled. Jonas and I'll sleep out here, and we'll send John over to his friends for a night or two. Mark can go in with Mom and the girls. See?"

"Benji, you're an angel!"

"Not really, but since you've almost attained that status in our eyes, we can't afford to turn you away." He chuckled, and his sister smiled slightly.

"But I didn't tell you anything! How did you know?"

"You're not flighty. You have valid reasons for the choices you make. And," his eyes twinkled as he added, "I happen to know Dad pretty well, too. We've crossed words many times. I could have turned bitter, but I figure life's too short for that. So, let's get on with your story. Why did you leave the convent?"

Anne found it easy to talk to Benji. He laughed at the idea of her life being in shambles. "Nonsense!" he said. "Look at all your skills—seven languages, the advantage of living abroad, as well as the discipline of convent life. I'd love to have you tutor my children!"

Benji rose and walked over to the magnificent gardenia bush. Picking a prime flower he presented it to his sister with a debonair bow. "Anne," he said, "this is what you are—beautiful and fragrant. There isn't a crooked thought within you."

She laughed, even while wiping tears, but this time they came from new hope. "Benji! You've struck it! Tutoring! I'd love that. But how do I get a job?" She tucked the flower in her hair and continued, "Since I've laid aside a nun's habit, I might as well enjoy flowers in my hair like the other ladies."

Benji grinned, and taking his seat again said, "Now that's more like it. I can't have you weeping around my house. Here you can laugh and love like the rest of us."

"I won't forget what you've done for me today. Now, Benji, how and where do I begin tutoring?"

After a moment's reflection he said, "We'll place an ad in the *Madras Daily*. That covers several large cities in the southland.

Something is bound to open up. Now, with your training in public relations, you write up something and I'll put it in."

"Oh, but that'll be expensive. I don't have the money."

He grinned and rubbed his hands together, then said, "I'll pay the bill, and when you can return the money, well, we'll talk about it then."

"Oh no, Benji, you're too kind."

"Not at all. I consider it an investment. You have to learn to gamble a bit. See? You're offering your tutoring skills in return for board and room and a bit in hand. That's fair enough. But beyond that, you're investing yourself in young people. Anne, that's tremendous! Most people want to live only for themselves. They haven't learned to reach out to others and make them happy."

"You have," she murmured.

"Pure selfishness," he responded with a grin. "I've always had a soft spot in my heart for my baby sister. Now I'm investing you into the lives of other young people. I should thank you for the chance."

She laughed. "I'll never forget what you've done for me today, Benji. I hope I can meet your expectations." She took a paper and pencil from her handbag and began writing.

Three mornings later, just before dawn, the Madras Express rolled to a stop in front of Coimbatore's bustling railway station. Within ten minutes eager boys waiting around the van of the *Madras Daily* grabbed their piles of newspapers to distribute throughout this industrial city. Krishna, a skinny twelve-year-old with torn shirt and faded pants was rudely pushed aside but finally picked up his pile and started off on his bicycle. His route took him into the heart of town, past the cloth merchants' shops. He hastened, hoping that nice Mr. Khan was waiting as usual.

Ali Khan, a Muslim merchant of modest means, dressed in white shirt and pajamas, with a white embroidered cap on his thinning hair, unlocked the sliding doors that opened onto the city street. He cleared the cloth covered platform of yesterday's litter, straightened the bolts of cloth on the shelves, and placed his money box, pad, and pencil conveniently. Then settling himself cross-legged on the platform, the merchant anticipated Krishna's coming. When the boy came by and threw the paper in, the man said, "Hello, Krishna, how's your mother?"

"Thank you, sir. Some better, but the doctor says she must have milk."

"Good idea, my boy. Here, take this *rupee* and buy her something special for lunch today."

"Oh, sir, you are too kind."

With a warm feeling inside, the man smiled and said, "Don't mention it. If there's anything I can do, just let me know." He nodded, and the boy hastened on with a wave of the hand. The man flipped through the pages, barely noting headlines. Only politics, he mused. He could read that at leisure, but now he must search the wanted ads. Day after day he looked in vain for someone to replace their beloved Ammachi. Not that he felt she shouldn't take responsibility for her ailing parents, but her going left a big hole in their family life. Why, she had cared for the boys ever since they were born, and now they were ten and twelve years of age. The merchant frowned. Shamir, his eldest, the same age as Krishna? But what a difference in status! Shamir and Yusuf never went to bed hungry. Ali Khan was sure Krishna often did.

Well, Krishna's mother would have a better lunch today, and milk. Praise be to Allah. Now he must see what he could do for his boys. The merchant flipped the pages of the newspaper. Then he saw it, words that stood out because of their simplicity and strength: "I can teach your children seven languages. I am a middle-aged woman needing a good home. I have public relations experience and extensive travel in my background."

The merchant took off his embroidered white cap, pushed his hair back, then replaced the cap, a gesture indicating deep thought. Hmmm . . . looks promising, he mused. He sighed, then muttered, "Don't know if we'll ever find anyone to replace good old Ammachi. But then, the will of Allah be done. Let me give this a try." Pulling pad with attached pencil toward him he noted the box number and wrote that very day for an interview.

Two days later Benji tossed several letters onto Anne's lap as she sat on the back verandah with Suzy. "Your ad's bringing response," he observed, chuckling. "We've got a VIP in our midst. Look, a convent . . . a private school . . . and. . . ."

"Nonsense," she said with a smile. "Deliver me from any more institutions! I could go back to the convent any day. Now, let's see. . . ." She held another up and scrutinized the envelope. "Ali Khan, Cloth Merchant, Coimbatore. Now, that's different." She tore the letter open and perused it quickly, then said, "I think I'll give it a try."

"What is it, Anne?"

"Private home . . . Muslim . . . cloth merchant in Coimbatore."

"Muslim?" Suzy looked skeptical. "Do you want to live in a Muslim home?"

"Why not? It will be safe, and surely different. I think I'll enjoy being hidden for awhile, time to reconstruct, you see."

"But Coimbatore's terribly dirty with all those cloth mills. The noise . . . the traffic. Likely the family lives above the shop," Suzy continued. "Now, if you'd get a nice school, you'd have a quiet compound and private quarters."

Benji chuckled, then commented, "Let her try it, Suzy. She has a flair for the unusual. And who knows what God is doing? Maybe that Muslim home needs her. If so, our faithful Lord will take care of her."

Anne gave her brother a grateful look and made preparations for the trip.

The next evening when she stood with small suitcase in hand in front of Ali Khan's shop she wondered whether she had chosen aright. Indeed, it looked as though the living quarters were on the second and third floors. And, as Suzy had said, this most surely was a noisy crowded street. Cyclists, rickshaws, pedestrians, trucks, busses, and hand-pushed carts vied with slow moving oxcarts for right-of-way on this bazaar road. If the family lived here, well, she might as well forget about quiet gardens and cloisters!

Anne sighed as she entered and asked for Mr. Khan. A half-dozen customers turned to look at the sweet-faced lady dressed in white, wearing a silver cross on a chain around her neck. They gave way as Ali Khan emerged from an inner office, and with a bow asked her to follow him upstairs to meet his wife and family.

The stairs were rather dark and narrow, but the opening of the door into a spacious room caused her to breathe a sigh of relief. Two windows and a door opened onto a closed-in verandah that faced the busy street. One end of the room held a dining table and chairs, with refrigerator set prominently in the corner. The other end of the room boasted a dark red oriental rug on the floor, an easy chair padded with black vinyl, and a bed-length divan covered with another oriental rug. Mr. Khan motioned his guest to the easy chair. "Please wait," he said. "I will call my wife and family."

Anne glanced quickly around the room. She missed the usual array of family pictures and certificates. Instead, a magnificent wall hanging depicted a forest scene. Several gaudy calendars advertising medicines hung by the kitchen door. A delicately carved teakwood screen with four panels formed a natural division between living and dining room. And on the floor, by the divan, stood a *hookah*. The nun wondered whether Ali Khan smoked it, or was there an old man here who bubbled away each evening on his tobacco?

Within moments, however, her attention turned to the family. Two boys bounded in to sit with their father on the divan. An elderly woman with a younger woman and child of about five clustered around the teakwood screen, curious but obviously shy. Ali Khan laughed and said, "You may come out. Our guest is a lady."

They approached noiselessly, barefooted. Young Mrs. Khan wore a light green tunic with matching pajamas, called *salwarkameez*, with a green filmy scarf around her neck. The older lady's white *saree* was neatly tied. Each bowed, then retreated to the safety of the screen, little Sunili firmly holding to her mother's shirt.

The boys began asking questions. "You know seven languages? Papa says maybe you'll teach us."

"Which languages, miss? Did you travel a lot?"

"Yes," Anne said with a smile, "Europe, Australia. . . . So I'll be happy to teach you what I know."

"She's nice, isn't she?" Shamir observed to his father.

"Another Ammachi, Papa!" Yusuf said with a grin.

"Very good, very good." Ali Khan rubbed his hands together with satisfaction. "We'll call you Ammachi, too [honorific form for "Mother"]. Yes, yes," he continued, "my sons need a broader outlook. I want them to travel, to learn, to see the world someday. All they know is India. Yes, it will be good."

"I will do my best, sir," Anne said. "But you understand, Mr. Khan, I'm not a Muslim. I am a Catholic nun. You don't mind?"

"Not at all, not at all. My father—bless his memory—taught me to see all as brothers. Ammachi, the boys attend morning school at the mosque, and the Mulvi Sahib sees to their religious training. We will be happy to have you do the rest. You, too, will bless them with what you have learned."

"Oh, thank you, Mr. Khan. I appreciate your confidence."

"Don't mention it. Now, about your quarters. Will you want to eat alone, or with the family?"

"Preferably on my own since I'm under doctor's orders and have a special diet. Otherwise I would be in the convent, but my health broke."

The women glanced at each other quickly, then smiled. Yusuf ran over, pulled at Anne's hand and said, "Ammachi, you can do your own cooking upstairs like our other Ammachi did."

Everyone laughed, and Ali Khan said, "Well, boys, it's time for a tour of the house, isn't it? I hope your new tutor likes us as well as we like her." Everyone nodded, and Anne felt a warmth springing up inside. Benji must be praying for me, she decided. His prayers are so personal, as though he actually knows God. Now mine . . . I wouldn't dare approach our Lord like my brother does. I'd be afraid!

Benji's last words came to mind as he saw her onto the train. "Remember, Anne," he said, "you're precious in God's sight. I know he has a perfect plan for you. I sense peace in your going to Coimbatore. But you know, if things don't work out, you can come home any time. We'll always make room for you."

"Bless you, Benji," she said, wiping tears. The whistle blew, the train began to move, and she could see her brother running alongside, saying, "Anne, God loves you, and so do we."

If only he could see her now, the nun thought with a hint of smile. Shamir grasped one hand, Yusuf the other. They wanted her to see the schoolroom first, then the apartment. The rest of the family followed, but the boys did the talking.

"See, Ammachi?" Shamir smiled broadly as they entered the glassed-in verandah. "We have a blackboard, and desks—just like a real schoolroom!"

"Yes," Yusuf added breathlessly, "and we come home at noon after going to our other school each morning. Ma gives us a hot lunch."

"Then we rest from one o'clock until two . . ."

"And have school here from two until five."

"I see, I see," Anne said with a broad smile.

"Let's see if your new Ammachi likes her quarters," the boys' father suggested. Everyone climbed the circular stairs, even petite Sunili who clung to her mother's long shirttail, then peeked shyly from behind Grandma's white cotton *saree* when they reached the top. The entire family wanted their guest to like her new home.

When Anne stepped onto the spacious rooftop, her eyes widened in pleasure. She saw an inviting courtyard with potted palms and flowering plants surrounded by a six-foot wall that ensured privacy from neighbors. Ali Khan noted Anne's surprise. Rubbing his hands together in a pleased gesture, he said, "I thought you might like a garden, Ammachi. We have many more plants in our private courtyard downstairs, and tomorrow our servant boy can bring some of my prize roses for you to enjoy. He'll take care of them, too, and do your cleaning and sweeping each day."

"Oh, Mr. Khan, that's too much," the nun said with that warm feeling inside.

"Not at all. We want you to be happy." He took a key from his bunch that hung at his waist, and bending over, opened the lock that held the screen door. "Too many flies," he muttered. "I think you're like the other Ammachi. She was very clean." He threw the door open and they entered.

Pulling the brocade dark red curtains back from glassed in windows and French doors, he stepped back and said proudly, "Your new home, Ammachi. I hope you like it."

An all-purpose room with a kitchenette at one end and attached bath at the other had been furnished with dining table and chairs. An apartment sized fridge stood in one corner; a teakwood carved screen, this one having three panels instead of four, separated the bedroom from the rest of the apartment. Recessed shelves would hold the precious library Anne hoped to build. She could see herself seated in the patio outside, or here at this pleasant study desk, writing. That easy chair needed a table lamp. She must get that with her first paycheck!

It was more, so much more, than she had imagined or even dared to dream. Had God prepared all this for her? Benji would say so. Anne drew a deep breath.

The family waited her response anxiously. "It's all right, Ammachi?" Ali Khan asked.

"More than adequate—private bath, kitchenette, even a garden. How can I thank you, Mr. Khan? I'm very pleased."

"Then we'll go over the terms of the contract tomorrow morning, but for tonight, you are our honored guest. The bed is ready for your convenience, and I hope you will eat dinner with us?"

"Thank you, you are too kind."

Young Mrs. Khan spoke for the first time, "Stay and rest now, Ammachi. Yusuf will call you when dinner is ready. Shamir, you go and bring her suitcase."

# Discovery

The sound of someone gargling, spitting, and coughing awakened Sister Anne in the early dawn on that first morning. Coming out of sleep in which she dreamed of being in the convent, the noise seemed alien, harsh. Anne turned over, trying to focus thoughts and consciousness, then realized the continuing noise came from across the wall. So, she had neighbors? An elderly man and wife? A medic or aspiring business man not yet financially capable of moving to a better apartment? Where was she? Ah, yes, on the third floor of Ali Khan's home.

Other noises penetrated, some familiar, some strange. The raucous cawing of crows reached her. Among all of God's feathered creatures were there any more demanding than these infamous, black-coated thieves? With a smile Anne began listening to other sounds—the honking of horns as trucks and busses vied for right-of-way, the grinding of motors, the shrill whistle of a factory calling workers to the early morning shift. Her imagination visualized the day progressing, with other sounds becoming familiar—the cry of the vendor, shrill voices of children, the screech of oxcart wheels.

A glance at her travel alarm made the nun jump out of bed. She had overslept! Dressing quickly, she pulled a small table and chair outside, and as she did so strong odors wafted on the morning breeze—the tangy whiff of a cowdung fire, the stronger hint of curried potatoes and frying fish, the tantalizing smell of strong coffee. It must have come from across the wall, Anne decided. Suddenly feeling hungry, she wondered whether she should go downstairs, but since the Khans hadn't mentioned morning routines, Anne hesitated. Perhaps it would be better to let Mrs. Khan make the first move this morning.

About seven o'clock, after having spent an hour in meditation, the nun heard the stairway door opening. Mrs. Khan called, "Ammachi, Ammachi, may I come?"

Anne looked up from her prayer book and said with a smile, "Good morning, Mrs. Khan. Please do. . . . Oh, how good of you. You carried a tray up those steps?"

Her companion laughed lightly and said, "I'm quite used to it. We've used these quarters for guests since the other Ammachi left."

"It's beautiful here," Anne murmured, pushing her books aside to make room for the tray.

"I thought I'd have to waken you. Please forgive me for not coming sooner. We should have set a time."

"No harm done." Anne noted the lady's dark red *sal-warkameez*, her jet-black hair tied in a knot at the nape of her neck. The faint fragrance of spice, or was it perfume, suggested Mrs. Khan was fastidious.

Her dimples played across her pleasant features, and she asked, "Did you sleep well, Ammachi? I do hope the Mulvi Sahib didn't waken you with his early morning call to prayer."

Sister Anne laughed. "It would have been good if he did, Mrs. Khan. . . ."

"Miriam," her companion said wistfully. "I like my name, but I never hear it. Would you mind using it when we're alone?"

"Of course," Anne said, giving her a quick glance. "Miriam is much nicer than calling you Mrs. Khan. Let me get you a chair. You've brought breakfast?" Anne took a deep whiff, then said, "Let me guess . . . *idli-sambar*?"

"Ma's best," the younger woman conceded. "Don't bother about the chair. I'm quite used to standing when my family eats."

"Of course . . . but if we're friends, I'd like to have you sit with me, Miriam. Here, you take this chair, and I'll get another."

"No, no! I'll get it! You're our guest."

"You win, but next time you'll be my guest, won't you?"

Before Miriam Khan left, Anne sensed a bonding with this quiet little lady. Was God sending her a younger sister, something she had never known?

Days and weeks progressed rapidly for Anne with tutoring in French and Spanish as her initial challenge. The boys loved their new Ammachi. Little Sunili, however, still clung to Grandma's *saree* or her mother's shirt rather than coming to the nun. And after trying daily to make conversation when Anne went early to the Khan's apartment for tutoring the boys, the nun soon learned that Miriam Khan lapsed into a completely secondary role when with husband or mother-in-law, or even with her daughter. The only time Anne and she could talk freely were those rare moments when the younger woman climbed the circular stairs on one pretense or another and they were alone.

Anne puzzled over this for weeks. One Friday evening while searching the radio dial for good music, she stopped. A mellow contralto voice caught her attention. She fine-tuned the program to hear the speaker say, "Look, my sisters, have you ever considered what the Lord Jesus Christ has done for us? We're not second-class citizens! We can go to schools and get a college education. We can enter areas of community life, give our service to the uplift of mankind. Think of Sister Teresa."

Anne was entranced. Who was this speaker, and what station was this?

"What right do I have to say this?" the lady continued. "Well, in case you just tuned in, I'm Sister Grace Lee Vanniasingham from FEBA India. I'm a retired principal of a girls' college in Jaffna, Sri Lanka, and now live in Bangalore. This city is filled with coeducational schools. Who began giving girls an education? The Christians. And why? Because Jesus Christ places a personal value on each and every one of us. I don't know who you are, but one thing I know—in God's eyes you're important! He loves you!"

Anne wiped a hot tear with the end of her *saree*. Why couldn't she turn this off? Why did she want to listen? Benji had told her the same thing, but Dad's words kept resounding in her mind night after night. "You are a sinner! You have broken your vows!"

"Oh, God," Anne moaned, "why do I have to hurt like this? Why do you follow me even here, in this little haven I've found where I can get away from everything and everyone?" She took a deep breath, but try as she might, she couldn't bring herself to turn to another station.

A touching song in Tamil followed, a song about Jesus' love. Then the warm contralto voice came on saying, "I'm sure at times all of us feel like we're not worth noticing. Perhaps you're trying to hide away like the Samaritan woman in our story. Women seldom go to the village well at high noon, do they? No, they like to meet others, to take advantage of the early morning coolness, to get as near the head of the line as possible. Why, you know how to place your gleaming brass vessel in line while you go off for a quick cup of coffee!" Sister Grace laughed, and Anne laughed with her.

The message concluded with the compassionate voice saying, "Have I told you truths you already know? Maybe you've known about Jesus Christ all your life. Maybe you've grown up in a religious home, and you know how to say your prayers and go to church. But it hasn't made any difference?" Sister Grace paused, then added warmly, "Let me tell you why, friend. We'll talk about that tomorrow, and do remember my offer to correspond with you. Here is the address."

Anne puzzled when she heard the station announcement. The program came from FEBA Seychelles, out in the Indian Ocean, but Sister Grace gave a Bangalore address. And she had said she lived in Bangalore. Perhaps she was there even now?

For the next five years Sister Anne listened to what she called the FEBA voices. Mornings and evenings she soaked in the music and messages, even finding broadcasts in French to the island of Mauritius.

This daily exposure effected some gradual changes, even as the gentle rains soften the earth. Harsh, bitter feelings gave way to noting down the contents of those messages that meant a great deal to Anne, particularly Sister Grace's. The quality of love, of caring that came through in each voice particularly spoke to the lonely woman in her apartment in Coimbatore. Often she felt like taking the overnight train to Bangalore to see if it was true, but the thought of another disappointment like that received at her own father's hand kept her from it. She contented herself with writing for program guides, and followed them avidly.

About four and a half years had passed since Anne had joined Ali Khan's family. Shamir was ready for college. Yusuf excelled in sports and loved to speak French and German. Little Sunili had conquered her initial shyness, and upon making friends with their new Ammachi found she, too, could learn to read and write. She often climbed those circular steps to the rooftop apartment to sit with Ammachi and listen to the FEBA voices that told about Jesus. The girl's penetrating questions embarrassed the nun. To Anne, religion was intended to be a completely personal affair. How could she talk about it to anyone, especially to an eager ten-year-old?

The nun evaded Sunili's questions, yet even in doing so felt a sense of inadequacy and emptiness. She spent extra time in prayers and meditations, but nothing satisfied. One Thursday evening about nine o'clock, Anne prayed spontaneously, "Lord Jesus, I don't know how to do this, but may I come as my brother Benji does? Please show me what I lack. I feel so empty, so lost."

Her hand flipped on the radio dial, set to FEBA Seychelles. An English program came on, with scintillating music filling her quarters, a rousing melody talking about joy in serving Jesus. Joy? Anne knew only heaviness. Where did they find this joy?

The preacher had one of those FEBA voices—caring, reaching out. Anne listened. "God isn't a policeman, monitoring your every thought in order to condemn you. He isn't an irate schoolmaster who confronts you with your shortcomings, my friend. No! The Lord Jesus Christ tells us he is a loving heavenly Father, one who cares so deeply about having sons and daughters that even before the world began, God provided a plan: His beloved Son, born of a virgin, came to be the perfect Lamb. Jesus is your Savior, friend, and you can trust him completely to lead you to God." There was more, and for the first time Anne began to see.

I've known about Jesus Christ . . . but have I known him? Benji does. He talks to him every day. I try to, but I don't have any confidence that he hears me. What's wrong?

The choir began to sing, "'Tis so sweet to trust in Jesus; just to take him at his word; just to rest upon his promise; just to know, 'Thus saith the Lord.'"

Trust? That's commitment! Letting yourself go, like Sunili letting go of her mother's shirttail and coming to me when I held out my arms, the nun mused. How foolish I've been. I haven't trusted. I've feared, like a little five-year-old when I tried so hard to win her.

Sister Anne began to laugh, a joy springing up inside as she raised her arms and said, "Lord Jesus, I trust you! You're my Lord and Savior. I don't need anything or anyone else. You're my sufficiency." She turned to her prayer book and began reading beautiful words that exalted God. How had she missed them before? Then she realized—they hadn't changed! She had! She was free, free to laugh, to love, to live! Oh, praise God forever. God had forgiven her sins, made her his own because his word is true. She must get a New Testament so she could read for herself. Her prayer book wasn't enough!

Anne became an avid student of the Bible, listening to the FEBA voices, noting down Scriptures, spending time meditating and praying. Joy lifted her along, and little Sunili found she could ask questions again.

Bubbling over with her new experience with God, the nun decided to attend services in the Catholic cathedral next Sunday. She met a former acquaintance, and that led to her finding more friends with whom to share her spiritual pilgrimage. But Anne came home disappointed. They simply didn't understand! She must pray for them.

Now she was ready to find Sister Grace Lee Vanniasingham. The next weekend Anne traveled to Bangalore, attending the Catholic services in Da Costa Square. Next morning she found the FEBA India headquarters, but learned that the office was closed because it was a national holiday. She found her way over to Vishranti Nilayam, the mother house for the Sisters of the Church of South India. Sister Grace lived in the new quarters, Anne learned.

So the two ladies met, and for two hours shared together. It began a friendship that continued over the years. Anne had made a tremendous discovery—she now belonged to the family of God.

## *Learning to trust*

The coolie tucked Anne's neat bedding roll and small suitcase under the train seat in the ladies' compartment in third class. Mr. Khan, hovering near, paid the porter, then turned to the nun as she took a seat by the window. "Will you be comfortable?" he asked. "This becoming a religious mendicant, Ammachi, may be admirable, but it's dangerous to say the least. Do you have any money?"

Anne laughed and replied, "Yes, I have some. As for the future—money, along with everything else, will be my Lord's concern, not mine."

"But what will you eat? Please let me know if you need help," the cloth merchant pleaded. "I'll send you money. Why, you're part of our family!"

"Thank you, Mr. Khan." Anne turned to Miriam Khan and her children standing on the Coimbatore Railway station platform.

"We wish you would stay," Miriam said softly, wiping a tear. She stood near the window, a shrouded figure in her black *boorka*. Mr. Khan joined his sons while Sunili clasped her mother's hand.

Anne smiled and responded gently, "Thank you, my dears. You've given me a beautiful home just when I needed it. Please don't grieve; I'll come back for mail. But I must go now. My Lord Jesus is calling to literally follow him."

The guard waved his green flag, the train whistled, and passengers standing outside rushed for the open door. Anne leaned out and waved to her benefactors as the train slowly moved down the long station platform. She saw them huddled together, a Muslim family whom God had used to shelter her. Why?

Pulling her small suitcase from under her seat, Anne took out some writing paper and a pen, and using the suitcase as a table, wrote, "Dear Sister Grace, now my address is c/o station platform! After months of inner conflict, I've left the comfort and security of a home and job to wholly follow the Lord. My friends think me unbalanced, crazy! They're sure I'll starve, but I know the Lord will care for me.

"Why this drastic step? I am learning to trust. The Holy Spirit has shown me I must enter a new school of discipline, one in which I have no roof, no security. I must represent my Lord in a new way.

"I believe my first stop will be Goa. Every time I see European hippies dabbling in Eastern philosophies, I feel I must tell them of Jesus, my Lord. I don't know where I'll sleep, or what I'll eat, but I look to the Lord to supply all my needs including an iron stomach! I know my FEBA family will pray for me. Do continue to write to my Coimbatore address. With much love, your little sister, Anne."

She had embarked on her two-year adventure of "trust."

Londa Junction! Perhaps its only significance came from the small train that ran daily to and from Panjim, Goa's capital city. As Anne walked its platform, carrying her bedding roll and suitcase, people turned to stare. Single women could be suspect, she reflected.

The mainline train for Bombay left noisily, and with it life on the station platform muted to a forlorn whisper. Anne crossed to the small line, then found a place on the train bound for Goa. It was early morning, time for breakfast. A passing vendor advertised his wares in dreary monotone.

"Come here," she called in Tamil, but the man looked at her blankly. Why hadn't she learned either Kannarese or Marathi, she wondered. Anne signalled the man to bring his large tray over to the window. By using sign language she bought some hot curry with Indian bread and finished off with a cup of steaming hot tea.

Then the nun drew her English New Testament from her shoulder bag and began to read. A Portuguese lady, middle-aged and grey-haired, watched her closely.

"Are you a Catholic nun?" Madame Estelle asked in English. Her companion looked up and said, "Yes, why?"

"I saw your silver cross and book."

"Yes, but at the present I'm an itinerant missionary. And you?"

"Retired, living near my sister on the home place ten miles north of Panjim. I'm returning from Bombay. Where are you going?"

"To Goa, for my first visit."

"Is that a New Testament, Sister?"

"Yes, do you have one?"

"No, but I read a bit from a copy that guests left on the living room table one day last Christmas. One couple with four girls came from Delhi, another with two children from Mussoorie, and a third from Bangalore. We had a party!"

"Do you regularly keep guests?"

"Not usually. But I needed extra cash to fix up the house, so I advertised. I've got the home place, you know—a fine house with thick mud walls. It dates back two hundred years!"

"Really?"

"Yes, back to the Portuguese. Plenty of room since my sister moved into her own house when she got her pension money." She hardly paused, then added, "They were interesting, those paying guests. One of the men came down with jaundice."

"That's too bad," Anne mumbled, wishing the woman would let her read. However, other interruptions occurred with the blowing of the whistle, the excitement of the train leaving Londa Junction. Passengers shouted goodbyes to their friends, and as the train gathered steam they finally settled down to reading or talking. One group of men got out a pack of cards and started a game at the other end of the compartment.

Anne tucked her New Testament into its accustomed place in her shoulder bag, and Madame Estelle took up the story where she had left off. "Those guests—you know, I liked them, Sister. The young man from Delhi—well, he plays the guitar and sings." She frowned slightly, then said, "I think he's Irish," then shaking her head added, "beautiful tenor, yes . . . Irish tenor. I took him and his wife, Maureen, and the girls to the Catholic orphanage to present a program. Yes, Sister, we had a marvelous time."

Anne sat up with interest. "His name was Jim?"

"Why, how did you know?"

"Jim and Maureen Hunter?"

"Yes, yes, that's right. Delightful people—so full of joy."

"Hmmm . . . and another couple came from Bangalore?" Anne chuckled. "I can venture a guess on them, too."

"You can? How do you know?"

"Let me try . . . elderly . . . she has white hair, and they're Americans, but they've lived in India a long time. How did I do?" Anne's eyes twinkled.

Madame Estelle clapped her hands together with delight. "Perfect! Imagine you being able to do that. How did you know, Sister?"

Anne laughed, took some wool and knitting needles out of her shoulder bag, and began casting on stitches for a sock. Her companion watched with interest. Anne answered, "How did I know? That's easy. They belong to each other. They're part of FEBA India, my special friends. I listen to them regularly over the radio."

"You do?"

The nun nodded and said, "Every day. By the way, how long did you say the group stayed?"

"The elderly people came for one week, the others stayed a fortnight. But, as I said, one of the men had hepatitis, so it wasn't a pleasant vacation for him."

By this time the little train chugged its way through the coastal range of mountains. Arid highlands now turned to heavy jungle growth, scenic waterfalls, and rugged terrain. As it puffed onward through tunnels and sleepy villages, Estelle and Anne's conversation deepened. The nun sensed a very lonely woman reaching out for friendship.

"Where will you stay?" the Portuguese lady asked. "You're a missionary? You'll likely go to some convent or church?"

"No, I don't think so, not this time. I'm looking for French hippies. I hear they congregate on Goa's fine beaches."

Madame Estelle looked grim as she replied, "One beach anyway. I don't think you'll enjoy their company. Our government is fed up with them."

Anne looked up with interest. "Oh? Why?"

"Drugs . . . and bathing in the nude! We call them starkys."

Anne chuckled and commented, "Apt name. Why do they choose Goa?"

"Beautiful scenery, warm climate, plus an abandoned monastery on the coast they've made their own, without anyone's leave, mind you!"

"Is that right?"

"I should know. It's only three miles from where I live!"

"How interesting. . . ."

Anne looked at her companion thoughtfully, but Madame Estelle continued, "I'd say they need some preaching! You want to see French hippies? I'm going to take you home with me!"

The day after their arrival, Sister Anne sought out the ill-famed beach. The gorgeous blue of the Arabian Sea stretched to the horizon. To her right, high on the bluff overlooking the beach, the abandoned monastery stood etched boldly against a cloudless sky. Palm trees and white soft sand lured tourists, some Goanese, but mainly starkys.

Anne spread the rug Estelle had given her. Under a palm tree near the motel and restaurant at the northern end of the beach, Anne began reading her French New Testament aloud. Her radio and shoulder bag sat on the mat beside her.

Several groups of European young people sauntered by. They looked at the Indian lady wearing a white *saree* and silver cross, slowed their pace, but went on. But after awhile three young people approached. "Where did you learn our language?" a bearded young man, sun tanned and bare to the waist, asked.

"In France," the nun said with a smile.

His two companions, both girls, giggled. The flaxen haired one asked, "Where in France?"

"Paris, in a Catholic convent."

"Ooh, Paris, that's my home!" She plopped onto the mat beside Anne and said, "I'm Lisa, and these are my friends, Marie and Pierre."

"And I'm Anne." She looked at the two who were still standing and said, "Come, friends, you might as well share my blanket." Marie, dark haired and willowy, contrasted with petite Lisa's fragile beauty. She sat beside the others while Pierre stretched on the sand, his arm under his head for a pillow. White clouds floated above, and the air was balmy and still except for the screeching of seagulls. A coastal liner maneuvered into sight from around the promontory on which the monastery stood.

Anne breathed deeply. "What a glorious place!" she said. "It's my first visit to Goa. How about you?"

A quick glance passed among the three young people. Marie said casually, "Oh, we've been in and out several times. We like it here." The girls tittered at Pierre's warning glance.

Lisa, tying her blond hair into a knot, said, "Marie and I grew up together in France. We met Pierre here."

"Graduate studies took me to your beautiful land," the nun remarked. "What brought you to mine?"

Pierre ran his hand through his red hair and gave a whoop.

"Yippee, I'm tired of being dictated to by society!"

"Right on, Pierre!" Marie added, "Lisa and I couldn't take being ruled by our families and forced to attend church. So we've come to India to really live."

"Hmmm . . . that's interesting. By the way, what do you call living?"

"Throwing away a watch," said Lisa.

"Not being bothered by rules and regulations," Pierre remarked as he stretched and yawned.

"Doing what we please, when we please. That's life!" Marie concluded. All three laughed, then rose to their feet. But Marie asked, "Will we see you again?"

Anne drew a deep breath, then said, "Let's try. Look me up about this time tomorrow, and we'll chat some more." She wondered whether they would actually come, but she breathed an earnest prayer that their friendship might deepen.

When Anne returned from the beach about sundown, Estelle asked, "Well, Sister? Did you meet any French hippies? I hope they were properly dressed. . . ."

Anne chuckled, then said with a wide smile, "What's proper attire for a starky? I'd say they did very well. Both Lisa and Marie had on a minimum, but at least they had on something. Same goes for Pierre. I can't complain."

Madame Estelle looked at her in amazement. "You mean to tell me you made friends with some of that trash? You know their names?"

"Not trash, Estelle. God loves every one of them, and he helps me to see them through his eyes."

"Well I never!" The middle-aged, Portuguese lady stood in her kitchen with her hands on her hips and said, "What do you know? I think you must be a saint. First you tell me Jim Hunter's name, and now you talk about that riffraff as though they're friends!"

Anne laughed aloud, "I love the way you put it, Estelle. But let me assure you, I'm no saint. I'm just one of God's children interested in finding some others who are lost—like I was."

"You, Sister? But I thought you were a nun."

"I'll tell you my story some day. Right now I feel rather mucky, so let me clean up before you serve some of your delicious curry and rice." She turned and went to her room.

At the table that evening Anne said appreciatively, "I'm so glad we met on the train, Estelle. This is ever so much tastier than institutional fare. Delicious!"

"Thank you. I'm so glad to have someone to share my food. My sister lives near me, but she prefers her own establishment. So I get pretty lonely at times. By the way, Sister, I can't get over your meeting those French hippies."

"I met more than the three I mentioned. Actually quite a few asked me where I learned their language. And this afternoon two young people listened to my radio when I tuned to the French broadcast over FEBA Seychelles."

"But I didn't realize they carry French! I've been listening to the English ever since our FEBA friends were here."

The next day Marie, Pierre, and Lisa plopped themselves again on the sand near the Indian nun. It became a daily encounter. On the fourth day of their friendship Lisa remarked, "Anne, we've been discussing some of the things you've said. We thought the church a dead institution, but you're hipped on religion. Why?"

"Because of Jesus, Lisa."

"Why get excited about someone who died two thousand years ago?" Pierre asked. He stretched out on the sand and yawned. Let the girls follow this crazy lead if they wished, but count him out.

But the nun said with a playful poke, "Young man, don't go to sleep yet. I want you to listen to this."

He turned over, grinned sheepishly and said, "All right, mom, get on with it. I'm all ears!"

She read the story of the resurrection. Pierre blinked in astonishment, then asked, "How do you know it's true?"

Anne chuckled, then said, "Figure it out for yourself, Pierre. See if it hangs together. I'll give you a copy to take back with you. Talk it over with the girls. They're smart! And I promise to discuss it with you tomorrow morning."

Those daily challenges brought results. Over lunch, shared with the young people, they argued and questioned, but always listened quietly to Anne reading a portion of Scripture. Each day she left them challenged to search for themselves.

Ten days passed. Then Marie and Lisa came alone. "Where's Pierre?" Anne asked.

"He's found another gal," Lisa said with a grin. "We've said goodbye. We're not living his kind of life anymore."

"Why, Lisa?"

"We've decided to follow Jesus," the girl remarked, and Marie nodded with tears in her eyes.

"We're on our way home to France, Anne," she said. "We've come to say goodbye. Our visa runs out next week. You know, we expected to cross into Nepal again, as we've been doing. But . . . well . . . you intercepted us and brought us to Jesus. We've come to say thank you, Anne. Thank you."

## Anne fulfills the vow

Sister Anne rose from her wooden bench in the ladies' waiting room on a hot, humid night in Trichy, South India. The light of the early dawn began filtering through windows made opaque by dust and grime. Shrouded figures filled the lounging chairs, their faces covered because of mosquitoes that buzzed and sang. Table tops and floor space accommodated more sleeping women, children, and stacked luggage. A child turned, a baby cried. The mother quickly silenced the little one by breastfeeding her infant.

On the station platform outside life began to stir as coffee vendors fanned dying embers in their braziers with palm leaves, or blew through bamboo pipes. Filling their galvanized vessels with coal, they put the kettle on in preparation for the next train's arrival.

For Sister Anne, itinerant missionary, privacy had become a luxury of her past. However, she tried to preserve as much of the treasured commodity as possible. By rising before others she managed to bathe, wash clothes, and care for personal needs before the morning rush. Arrayed in her usual white with the silver cross around her neck, Anne would pay the room attendant a slight fee to care for her luggage while she sought a private spot for morning devotions. To Anne, meeting her Lord became her highest joy.

Sometimes it brought unusual results. One morning she received a strong impression while in prayer. Instead of going to the bazaars and village today, she should stay in the waiting room. Sure enough, an incoming train brought an influx of Indian pilgrims returning from a large religious fair. A wealthy mother and daughter, ascertained by their apparel and demeanor, sat near Anne, and from their conversation she gathered they had come back disillusioned. Anne told them of Jesus. Not only did the ladies listen but the mother impulsively handed Anne a roll of bills, saying, "You have helped me more than all the gurus I met. Please take this in the name of your God."

The afternoon train brought three European girls, who, like Anne, knew no other home in India than the station waiting room. When she heard them talking in French, she prayed for a chance to witness for the Lord, but they seemed preoccupied, eager to visit Meenakshi's temple in Madurai. Anne sensed a deep gulf between herself and them.

"Will I see them again, dear Lord?" She prayed desperately, "And if I do, how can I get through to them?"

"Yes, my child, five days from now the group will return this way, disappointed. They won't find peace worshiping any Hindu goddess."

"Dear Lord," Anne said, wiping tears as she lay on her mat under the fan in the waiting room that afternoon, "I must tell them about you."

"Then identify with them. Don't wash your clothes or hair for five days. Your cleanliness is a barrier, but if you do what I say, I'll open their hearts to your message."

"Dear Lord! You want me to stay here five days? Not wash my clothes! But look how grubby this place is! How can I stand it?" She turned her face to the wall lest others see her crying.

The inner voice continued, "Daughter, do it for me. I gave my back to be scourged, my head for a crown of thorns, my blood for your sins and theirs. Can't you forego your own personal habits of cleanliness to talk to these girls?"

"Yes, Lord, forgive my questioning. I'll do it . . . by your grace."

Sister Anne wrote her FEBA family about the experience. "I can't tell you how dirty I felt . . . not bathing for five days, letting my hair become stringy and grimy, filled with coal dust! I never want to do it again! But, dear Sister Grace, when those girls returned disappointed and disillusioned, they were ready to listen. I saw them off this noon on a train bound northward, and with them went a substantial amount of literature from my shoulder bag. I was able to buy it because of the gift that wealthy Hindu lady gave me five days ago. See? The Lord provides for my needs."

Anne's station platform experiences took her from Telugu country to the southern tip of India in those exhausting two years when she learned to trust. She wrote Sister Grace many times, knowing that the entire FEBA Staff in Bangalore would be praying for her. That undergirding strengthened her in many trying circumstances. The nun's little shortwave transistor radio remained her constant companion, assuring her she was not alone.

After her Goa experience Anne sheltered for a week or ten days in the quiet Christian Retreat Center in Andhra Pradesh and there revelled in finding others who knew her Lord. But the Spirit of God soon led Anne southward again to trek village trails.

One morning at a railway station, seated on a bench overlooking a mango grove, she heard the bazaar noises beckoning. But pushing them aside she prayed, "Where do you want me to go today, dear Lord?"

The directive came clearly, "To the gypsy village. They need to hear."

The day proved hot and dusty. After walking an hour on a road leading south, Anne pushed her neatly combed hair back and looked in some dismay at her clean white *saree*. At least it had been clean, she mused ruefully as she stopped to straighten the pleats. Then trudging the sandy trail, she wondered wearily whether that gypsy village lay around the next corner.

Yesterday, as she sought to witness to people gathered at a bazaar tea stall, a group of gypsies and their dancing bears suddenly disrupted the serious talk about God. Greatly disappointed at the interruption, Anne wondered whether the Lord might have a purpose in this encounter. She asked, "Where do you live?"

Learning the general direction, she turned to the owner of the tea stall and said, "I'll be going now, but thank you for giving me a chance to talk to you about the Lord Jesus."

"Thank you, Sister," he said with a smile. "You are welcome any time."

Now Anne prayed as she walked the dusty trail. Would the gypsies also accept her? She knew their nomadic lifestyle, but there the similarity stopped.

Ten minutes later the Tamilian nun neared the encampment of huts spread underneath some welcome shade trees, but the hovels seemed empty. Had she missed the Lord's cue? Where were the gypsies?

A sweet, clear voice singing a popular love song soared over the still air. Anne turned aside to see. A girl, aged about ten, skipped rope outside a shanty in the heart of the village. Her bright eyes scrutinized the newcomer, eyes twinkling with the joy of vagabond existence. What Anne saw, however, was a half-naked child—barefoot, hair falling every direction. The child is obviously happy, despite her lacking things others think so essential, thought Anne.

"You're really happy?"

"Oh, yes, Miss," the girl said, stopping momentarily to eye the newcomer with interest.

"What is your name?"

"Soma." She pushed her hair out of her eyes.

"Well, Soma, I think you have a beautiful voice."

"People tease me about my singing, but I don't care."

"Where has everyone gone? I see hardly anybody here."

The girl began skipping, counting, "One . . . two . . . three . . . four . . . five . . . six . . . seven . . . eight . . . nine . . . ten. . . ." Stopping and drawing a deep breath, she said, "We're gypsies, Miss, and they've taken the bears to the villages to dance for the people. They'll bring money back this evening to buy food. When we finish around here, we'll go somewhere else. I like it. It's fun!"

"But why didn't you go along, Soma? Don't you enjoy watching the bears?"

"Of course, but it's almost time for me to turn on the radio at my uncle's house. I want to learn some more songs."

The nun looked at her with interest. "Hmmm . . ." she said, "so you learn your songs from the radio?"

The girl resumed her skipping and counted, "eleven . . . twelve . . . thirteen . . . fourteen . . . fifteen. . . . Yes, Miss," she said as she stopped skipping and let her rope hang by her side. "My uncle, he's grouchy. See him sitting over there, under that big tree? He's watching me. He makes me pay money to listen to his radio."

The nun shifted her shoulder bag, heavy with literature. "You mean you have to pay your uncle to listen? But, why, Soma? And where do you get your money?"

"Oh, I save it. You see, when my brothers and sisters buy peanuts, I remember that learning songs is more important. My uncle won't let me listen unless I pay him. I tried to coax him to turn on the radio for me, but he won't. He says it takes money to buy batteries, so I pay him each time."

"Hmmm. . . ." Anne's thoughts whirled. Now she knew why the Lord had sent her today. She opened her shoulder bag, reached in and extracted a FEBA India Radio program guide. The child watched her.

"You like to learn new songs, Soma?"

The girl answered eagerly, "Can you teach me? I want to learn all the new songs. I love to sing."

"Of course, child. You sing very well, and you must keep on. I can't teach you a song today, but I'll do something better. I'll tell you where you can hear beautiful songs on your uncle's radio. Now, isn't that much better?"

"Where, Miss?"

"Right here. See, I'll mark it for you. Can you read?"

"No, but my uncle does. He'll tell me the right place."

"That's great. Now, child, remember to keep on singing, and if you listen every day to this station you'll hear many new songs. Thank you for singing for me. I think you do very well, Soma."

The girl clutched her precious paper, threw her rope down and ran to her uncle, shouting, "Thank you, Miss, thank you."

Anne walked on. The seed had been sown . . . the harvest would come. Less than a mile beyond the gypsy encampment she passed a Hindu Ashram, a spiritual life center. Anne stopped a moment at the gate and noted the well-kept appearance of the lodges and gardens.

Several weeks later the Tamilian nun again trudged that same trail. As she neared the shanty village where Soma lived, she wondered whether her singing friend had gone. Had she learned new songs? Songs of Jesus? "Please, Lord," Anne prayed, "I'd like to know, if you care to tell me."

Within moments Soma's clear, sweet tones floated over the midmorning air. Anne straightened, and smiled. She heard words describing the love of Jesus for a lost world. Soma and her uncle had indeed found FEBA Seychelles on their radio dial. The tiny seed Anne had planted would grow, and eternity would reveal the rest of the story. "Thank you, Lord!" Anne said as she trudged on.

Sister Anne drew a deep breath. This morning's directive demanded a whole new dimension of trust. Ever since seeing the Hindu Ashram the thought kept coming back to her, why not enter? That's where I'll find my hippies!

But another part of her kept saying, impossible! I'll be on the devil's territory! It's bad enough to leave home, security, and the love of understanding friends. How can I do this? I don't believe the Lord is asking it of me. Surely he loves me too much?

But the niggling thought kept surfacing as Anne contacted Christian schools in the area and told the teachers about the radio programs. True, she distributed many program guides and had opportunities to give her witness in many places, but always the call to minister to European hippies kept returning. Where better than in a Hindu Ashram? This morning's directive came loud and clear. Anne knew she must obey.

A young Indian disciple dressed in saffron robe answered the doorbell and invited her in. Mother Satyaraj (literally means "kingdom of truth"), couldn't be seen right now, he said, but an assistant would gladly show the visitor the grounds. Anne followed a young lady through quiet gardens bursting with color. Seekers of truth meditated here, Anne's guide said, and indeed, the nun saw them everywhere, some bowing to many idols placed in shrines throughout the gardens.

Completing the tour, Anne finally met Mother Satyaraj, an elderly Indian lady dressed, as were her devotees, in saffron robes. Her eyes were unusual, beautiful eyes that seemed to belong to a mystic. At the moment, though, they focused on Anne's face as this spiritual leader smiled inscrutably. The nun sensed that those black, dreamy eyes could also flash fire under provocation. White, wavy hair framed the oval face, and her strong, capable hands suggested one of noble birth, as did her well-built physique.

"Who are you?" Mother Satyaraj asked the newcomer.

"I was formerly a Catholic nun, but I left the orders to now become an itinerant, a searcher after truth."

"Oh? You want to stay here?"

"If you'll have me. I noticed, however, that you seem to have mostly Europeans."

"Oh, by no means! We do take them, as well as Indians, but, well . . . you see, our pilgrims don't usually have money. The others help maintain the work for those who can't pay."

"I'm afraid that I'm one that can't afford to pay."

"You're truthfully a searcher after truth?"

"Yes, mother."

"Who's your guru?"

"Jesus of Nazareth."

"You could have none better. Do you have a mantra?"

"Yes, mother."

"Then you may come. Where are your things?"

"At the railway station. If you will accept me without payment, I'll return by evening."

Mother Satyaraj shifted in her easy chair. "Very well," she said, "come by four o'clock so you can settle in before evening meditations."

"Thank you, mother. I'll hurry."

Anne had learned many lessons in trust during her station platform experiences, but this? She prayed as she walked, "Are you sure, Lord? I can't afford to make a mistake. By going into the Ashram I enter the very heart of Hinduism. Is that where you're sending me?"

Well, she reflected, she needn't return. She could take the train for another destination, or even go back to the Khans in Coimbatore. How could she face the rigors of again becoming a member of a rigid institution? Anne vacillated all the way throughout the four-mile journey.

But she had given her word! And the inner voice prodded, saying, "Daughter, I left heaven's glory and took the disguise of man so that I might bring the salvation of God. Are you willing to live among those who search vainly for truth, to show them my glory?"

By the time Anne reached the station she knew she must return. A new sense of inadequacy covered her, along with the assurance that the Lord would provide the enabling for the challenge ahead. She hired a rickshaw to hasten her return, and even experienced a rising sense of anticipation.

Left alone for an hour until time for evening meditation, Anne replaced her civilian garb with the saffron-colored blouse and *saree* she had been issued, careful, however, to keep the silver cross close to her heart. Her sparsely furnished room exhibited a large framed picture of Mother Satyaraj, the enlightened one. A printed set of rules hung by the door—certain hours for meditation, work assignment for non-paying residents, times for meals, and hours for silence. The nun smiled at its familiar overtones.

But she shuddered as she looked around. In her convent quarters she saw Catholic mementos; here, there were Hindu gods and goddesses. Whisking the memorabilia away into a bottom drawer, she prayed a sanctifying prayer over the room and said, "Lord Jesus, you are greater than all the forces here symbolized, and in the victory of Calvary I claim peace."

The gong for evening prayers sounded. Anne hastened to the audience hall where the devotees met twice a day with their spiritual leader. Seventy disciples took their places on grass mats, each assuming the lotus-like position. As Anne sat near the back, she noticed a number of Europeans scattered among Indian pilgrims. All bowed as Mother Satyaraj took her place on a slightly raised platform covered with a thick cotton pad.

She wore a look of peace and spoke in soft tones, her eyes half-closed, her brow bearing three white horizontal stripes. Her assistant, the young man whom Anne met first, led in singing songs of praise to their leader. Voices resounded through the room to the accompaniment of drums, flutes, and cymbals. Lyric followed lyric until Mother Satyaraj signaled she desired to speak. Her disciples leaned forward to catch every word.

"My children," she said in a dreamy tone, "all roads lead to God. He is all around you—in every tree, bush, and flower. He is above, and below, and within. Yes, within! The divine flame merely needs fanning, and this is your task. You must negate the infusion of all that binds—worldly concerns, the anxieties and frustrations that have driven you to seek peace. Let divine love flow unhindered through you to bless a needy world. Close your mind to all else and open it to the infinite."

This initiated a general chanting of mantras, some sedately, others in varying stages of ecstasy. Anne sat quietly among them, praying, "Jesus, Prince of peace, give me your peace."

Two Westerners glanced her way, and following evening prayers sought her out. The tall young man with wavy light hair asked, "You're new here?"

"I came this afternoon," Anne said with a smile. "And you?"

"We've been here for the last ten days," his companion said. "We're Mike and Bekky."

"And you can call me Anne. Where's your home?"

The petite brunette looked up at her companion and said, "Mike—he's from Jerusalem; me—I'm from New York. We're Jews. We met about two months ago and have been traveling."

Anne nodded. Their next question stunned her. "Where did you find your peace?" Mike asked, fingering his medallion.

"But how do you know I have peace?"

"From your face, Anne," he said. "You're not at all like the rest of us. Bekky and I have searched everywhere. Haven't we, Bekky?"

He turned to her, and she nodded, "Yes, Anne, from Kedernath in the Himalayas to the Godavari in the south. We've tried it all, then came here since Mother Satyaraj is so well known."

The silence bell rang at that point, and Anne promised hastily, "We'll talk tomorrow."

Bekky and Mike sought her out as she sat alone reading her New Testament in a corner of the gardens. "Who's your guru?" Bekky asked, plopping down on the grass.

"I wondered how soon you would ask," Anne said, chuckling. "You'll be surprised. I follow Jesus of Nazareth."

"You don't mean it!" the girl said, her black eyes flashing. Mike lay down beside her, and propping his head on his elbow looked up at Anne and asked, "You mean you don't worship Hindu gods and goddesses? And you're Indian? A pilgrim? A seeker after truth?"

"Exactly, my dears, that's what I'm telling you." She drew a deep breath and added, "Sometime I'll share my story with you, but first, fellow pilgrims, I'd enjoy hearing yours."

In the hour that followed before the evening bell rang, Anne listened to a story of fear, frustration, confusion. "We . . . we felt so alone, Anne, that we finally teamed up together two months ago, and I can't tell you. . . ." Bekky wiped a tear.

"Don't talk about it, dear," Anne said, caressing the saffron colored bandanna that hid the girl's short curly hair.

Mike spoke up. "I found her devastated, without money, and the fellow she was with, Anne, found another girl and left just like that! I couldn't stand it, so we've been friends ever since. I think the worst, though, was when we took a vow to gain peace and sold her beautiful black hair to pay for it."

"Where?"

"In a big temple in Telugu country . . . a long name," he said with a sheepish grin.

"Never mind the name. Tell me about the vow."

"Bekky's black hair, of which she was so proud, fell almost to her waist," Mike said. "And to think the priest asked for it!"

"To pay the vow, Anne," the girl said appealingly, stretching her hand out for understanding.

The nun nodded. "Never mind, it will grow again. I'm sorry, though, that you fell prey to a profiteering scheme."

"What do you mean?"

"That temple supplies human hair for wigs. It's big business."

"Really?" The girl looked dazed. "I didn't know."

"Yes," Anne said with a smile. "Your beautiful hair will likely land up in New York City, your home."

The young people looked at each other, and Mike said slowly, "Are you telling us the truth?"

Anne nodded, a hint of smile on her face.

"Bekky, I think we've been duped. Something tells me Anne's found what we need. I'd like to hear her story."

"Tomorrow, my dears," the nun said softly. "We must go to meditation now, but let me change your mantra. Say, 'Jesus, Prince of peace, give me your peace.'"

"Will it work?" Bekky asked, getting up and tying her bandanna more snugly.

"Try it, and let me know," Anne said as she stood and tucked her precious New Testament in the folds around her waist. They walked together toward the hall, with Anne in the middle.

The Jewish young couple left the Ashram within the week, but not before Anne led them to her Lord. When Mike reached

Jerusalem he wrote, "I want to thank you, Anne, for leading me to my Messiah. Would you believe I had to travel to India to find him? It's unthinkable, but true. Thank you, Anne."

Back in the bosom of her Muslim family in Coimbatore, Anne read the letter, wiped her tears and said, "And, Lord Jesus, I thank you for giving me a chance to pay my vow of gratitude to you. I've had a wonderful two years."

*A political procession in Calcutta*

# Aleyamma of Travancore

## *Herald of the dawn*

On a steamy summer evening in Kottayam, Travancore, city dwellers poured out of stuffy buildings to seek relief. The sun, no longer blistering, sank low on the horizon of the Arabian Ocean, and sweet breezes began to blow across the land.

People flooded the marketplace. Matrons gossiped or haggled over bargains, eager for the fresh fish of that day's catch. Children shouted joyously at the peanut vendor and the lure of brightly painted wooden toys, or maybe ribbons and bows. The passing gypsy with his dancing monkey caused all to halt their play to follow the newcomer.

In that same marketplace, white-haired elders hobbled along, leaning on their canes, eager to share news and views with like-minded friends. Politics sometimes claimed their attention, but more often they paused to decry the sad state of affairs among the insolent young.

Those same insolent young, on that steamy evening in Kottayam's marketplace in 1934, sought relief from boredom. Then, as now, many lounged around idly, seeking new causes with which to identify.

News from across the mountains said that the political movement for freedom from Britain's hold over India was gaining momentum. Mohandas Karamchand Gandhi's name kept recurring in the newspapers, but British India and its problems seemed very remote to this Malabar Coast region that had never known any rule except their own. Now, with revolution in the air, young men began talking Marxism, a chance to overthrow the Maharajah who ruled in lordly splendor in his capital, Trivandrum. No wonder their elders dubbed them the insolent young!

Processions occurred almost daily in Kottayam. One cause or another, espoused by concerned individuals, often ended in volatile and vehement declarations. Young men seeking white-collar jobs in this overcrowded state sought the excitement of changing the status quo just to escape boredom.

On this particular day a song wafted on the evening breeze as a procession approached. People stopped to listen, then ran to better see the group. Young men immediately stepped into the ranks of the marchers to be at the heart of whatever happened.

The crowd pressed in. This was no ordinary procession! About twenty young people surrounded a strikingly tall lady dressed in white. She looked to be about forty years of age, and was playing a tambourine and singing. Her face gripped the onlookers; radiance rested on her features, as though she saw into another world. To the accompaniment of an accordion, kettle-drum, and flute, she led the chorus of young people in hauntingly beautiful lyrics about Jesus.

The crowd pressed closer. The only religious music these Travancorians knew were the Syriac chants and liturgies used in their churches. They were proud of them, even though they couldn't understand a word, for the church maintained their time-given heritage. Hadn't St. Thomas come to India in 52 A.D. to establish it? Evidences in wayside shrines and cathedral-type structures abounded in and around Kottayam.

But why would anyone choose to bring religion into the marketplace? Only the priests intoned the great truths of the Christian faith, certainly not the laity! Who was this woman?

People listened closely, attracted by the lyrics. They hushed, straining to hear the sweet cadences rise and fall, this music that caught their hearts:

*Jesus is my friend, hallelujah;*
*He is my beloved.*
*Whatever my trials may be, yes,*
*Jesus is my friend, hallelujah.*

*There is a tree of alms whose branches never fade;*
*When there is no room in the inn, I sleep beneath its shade.*
*When I have no clothes and only rags cover me,*
*Even then I know that Jesus is my friend.*

*Jesus will give me a golden chain,*
*Not from the gold of this earth,*
*But from the gold of Zion's glorious streets,*
*Will come my chain of worth.*

Literally thousands followed the singers to the open fields of Baker's Square. There, packed body to body, they gave undivided attention for two hours of music, testimonies, and message. The sweet breeze of heaven swept over them.

Aleyamma Oommen and her evangelistic team stood on the second floor balcony overlooking the vast audience. Microphones had not yet been invented, so "repeaters" stationed themselves throughout the vast crowd. Each repeated the message, phrase by phrase. Song leaders pressed forward, seeking to capture the words and tune of each new lyric. They soon joined in, until the mass of listeners became one great chorus, singing the praises of God.

During a recent visit to Kerala, formerly known as Travancore until it joined the newly-formed Indian Republic in 1947, my husband and I, with our friend Mrs. Abraham, eldest daughter of Aleyamma, sought out Baker's Square. Chinnakutty eventually located the building on which verandah her mother and the team had stood in the Kottayam Crusades. The area, about five by twenty feet, was suitable for platform use. Some eight feet off the ground, it provided a vantage point from which to preach to the thousands listening in the fields below.

The verandah has now been bricked in to make an additional room, but the company's name, "Million and Company," still hangs above the door. An encroaching city now supplants the open fields. But standing there, one can easily reconstruct the scene as described by those who attended.

Mr. Thomas Mattai says, "The crusade I remember took place in Baker Square in 1934. I was an impressionable boy aged thirteen. In that crusade there were about twenty team members, including three sons and one daughter of Mrs. Oommen's."

I turned to my friend, Chinnakutty Abraham, eldest daughter of Aleyamma and our guide on this fact-finding mission, and remarked, "Three sons? That sets this crusade after Unni's return, doesn't it?"

The grey-haired business woman with the regal bearing smiled and said, "You're right, Sister Leoda. Unni had just been converted, and mother brought him with her to Kottayam to help establish him in his newfound faith. I'm sorry I missed being here."

"So you weren't the daughter Mr. Mattai mentions?"

Her black eyes twinkled as she responded, "Not I! I can't sing, but I can cook! Mother always left me with the household responsibilities until I married and moved with my husband to Cochin. My sister Lilly has a beautiful voice, so she was a member of the chorus."

"I see," I said, as I made notations in my journal.

Mr. Mattai intercepted, "I remember that crusade very clearly. All of us young people attended. We stood in the open square every evening from seven to nine o'clock, gazing upon Mrs. Oommen's glowing features. We thought she looked like an angel, and her messages and music won us immediately. She possessed a strong voice that carried far."

He paused, then said with a wry smile, "I'd say most of the people felt as we did, but there were hecklers to add spice. I remember the evening when one man called out during her message, 'So! The hen has begun to crow!'"

Mr. Mattai chuckled, then continued, "Mrs. Oommen didn't flinch, not for one moment! She turned his direction and said clearly, 'Morning is coming, my brother, and there is no cock to tell of the dawn.'"

"Ah, yes," Chinnakutty remarked with a smile. "That sounds like mother. God gave her special wisdom, but I happen to know her secret."

"What?" I poised my pen to write.

"We used to worry about her. She wouldn't eat, but fasted and prayed daily until time for the evening meeting. Only after the service would she take food. You know, we saw many miracles and hosts of conversions."

"Ah, I see," I said, as I wrote in my notebook. Who was this flaming prophetess who spoke of the dawn to a decadent, ritualistic society?

# Early years

She came of a long line of Christian workers and preachers from a delightful village in central Travancore, now known as Kerala, near the southernmost tip of India. Kodukulanji, the charming hamlet built on the side of a hill and valley five miles from the larger town of Chennganur, had known the gospel for the past 250 years when little Aleyamma came on the scene. The youngest of three children, born on January 29, 1895 to preacher Johannen and his lovely wife, Aleyamma, a teacher from the royal city, Trivandrum, little Aleyamma soon became the pet of the family.

Their uncluttered life centered around farming verdant rice fields and planting cashew trees and bananas among the ever-present palms. Johannen taught his son to fish, and John became adept in supplying his daily catch, often from the stream near the house, but sometimes from the backwaters and even from the not-too-distant ocean. John's mother fried the fish, and steamed, dried, and pickled it. Eaten with rice or tapioca from their farm, her curried dishes changed every meal into a celebration.

The preacher's family also treasured their coconuts. They drank the refreshing liquid from yet green fruit, and relished the tasty greyish-white meat when snacking. Big Aleyamma used coconut to flavor every curry, and in her leisure time wove palm leaf mats for household purposes. The wide fibrous leaves of the coconut palm also supplied thatching for roofs.

Twice daily the children placed the grass mats on the hard dirt floor, and squatted with their parents for morning and evening devotions. After singing lustily, they listened to Scripture and Bible stories. Then came prayer. Throughout, little Aleyamma's voice rose exultantly, and her parents encouraged her to take lead parts. Her unusual grace and beauty marked the child, as did her leadership qualities. In response, her family molded her with love, never with harshness.

Johannen's house was almost hidden by palms, barely a half-mile from the village. It boasted a front door painted bright blue, with hand-tooled vines and flowers embellishing it. The door still stands, as does the well at the back and portions of the original structure. One can easily imagine young Aleyamma chasing monkeys from grain drying in the sun, or feeding the chickens that wandered freely.

Kodukulanji is part of a tropical paradise, an area that has never known total crop failure. With torrid heat as the norm, and two annual monsoons, thick jungle pervades. Parrots and other exotic birds nested there; monkeys peered down from tree branches. The rhythmic rap of the woodpecker synchronized with frogs croaking and crows cawing. Bees hummed around giant sized plants and flowers, busily storing nectar amid a riot of color.

Sometimes brief storms lashed the countryside. Grey clouds chased across the sky as ominous thunder rolled. After the interlude of lashing rain, a cacophony of jungle sounds erupted with crickets vying for attention. That's the way it was in Aleyamma's day, and that's the way it remains.

In the cottage of the beautiful door, days and weeks passed quickly. Too often Johannen's wife struggled on alone while her preacher husband joined an English missionary, Mr. Pete, on evangelistic tours. John daily climbed the hill to the mission school, but it educated only boys, not girls. It had always been that way, and nobody tried changing the status quo. Not in Kodukulanji!

However, Aleyamma, educated in Trivandrum, felt strongly about teaching her two girls. How different her life in the city had been! Not only had she learned from the two English missionary ladies who lived in the royal city, but she had also taught in the prestigious Fort School for Girls they established. She sighed, and determined to talk her husband into moving his family back to Trivandrum. It happened when her youngest, little Aleyamma, was six.

## The royal city, Trivandrum

Travancore's capital city sat at the southernmost tip of India. Ruled by an enlightened Hindu Maharajah, this coastal kingdom had traded with other nations for centuries, yet never known foreign domination, not even the British. This may have been due to the formidable mountain barrier that protected the Malabar coast from the rest of the subcontinent.

Travancore's seaports, and that of its neighboring kingdom, Cochin, lay on the direct merchant routes between the Middle East and China. For thousands of years merchant vessels from distant nations brought gold coins to barter for peacocks, spices, apes, and ivory. Some treasures must have found their way to Solomon's court in Jerusalem!

This rich historical background is seen in Kerala today in fishing techniques from China, as well as upturned corners on rooftops. The Syriac liturgy is still used in the Syrian Orthodox Church that claims St. Thomas as founder in 52 A.D. Churches and shrines abound, bearing witness to this strongly entrenched tradition.

In Cochin one can see Vasco de Gama's grave in an ancient stone church dating back to the fourteenth century when Portuguese explorers imported Catholicism and left their mark on architectural designs.

With this awareness of worlds beyond the horizon, it's not surprising that Travancore's ruler paid an annual visit to the ocean to offer tribute to the gods of sea and sky. Nor is it amazing that he should welcome foreign visitors to his kingdom, whether entrepreneurs or missionaries.

Not all of his subjects shared his liberal views. After the Maharajah had established the school for girls within the fort walls, Namboodhri Brahmans resisted to the point of closing it without the Maharajah's knowledge, let alone consent. What happened then occasioned one of Travancore's favorite stories.

At the close of the rice harvests the great ten-day festival of Dusshera was at hand, a time for dancing and singing. "Bring the royal elephants," the Maharajah cried. "This procession to the ocean shall be one to remember!"

"Yes, your Majesty."

"And the cavalry, followed by the infantry. We shall show our military strength to friend and foe alike."

On the appointed day His Royal Highness and family rose early to worship at their private Hindu temple adjoining the palace. The procession then formed, with the elephants leading, rich in trappings of red and gold shimmering in the sun. The colors matched the scarlet uniforms of the *mahouts*, drivers who sat in front of *howdahs* that carried dignitaries of state under gaudy umbrellas. Next came the cavalry, then the infantry, platoon by platoon, foot soldiers with brave records.

At the very end of this impressive show, two lone figures trudged barefoot on fine white sand that had been spread for royal feet. The taller stood bare to his waist except for the sacred cord crossing his chest, but his cloth skirt gleamed with heavy gold thread. He wore a green cap and carried a shining sword. His younger brother, garbed similarly, carried a shorter sword and followed the king.

As they walked, a cat suddenly scurried across the road, immediately in front of the Maharajah. A coincidence? By no means, the king groaned. This bad omen portended great evil!

He reeled in disbelief. Why should this happen to him now? What had he done to displease the gods? His triumphal march degenerated into a penitential pilgrimage, even as thunder rolled in the distance. He hastened to the priests awaiting him at the ocean front and cried, "Why are the gods displeased?"

Silence. A cloud covered the sun, and the waves pounded.

"Speak, I command you!" The king shivered in the chill wind.

A Brahman stepped forward, bowing low. "Your Royal Highness," he began, "the gods are displeased because some of your subjects are opposing the two good ladies who came across the ocean to teach your daughters."

"What do you mean, opposing?" he shouted above the whistling wind. "Speak!"

"Please excuse me, but some Namboodhri Brahmans locked the door of the Fort School for Girls."

"Never! Who dares challenge my authority?"

An officer came forward even while the informer hastily slipped away into the crowds. "Your Honor," he said, "two foreign women are teaching your children about strange gods. Surely you don't desire it?"

Thunder rolled, and the wind intensified.

"See what you've done!" the king shouted. "The gods are angry! We're doomed!"

Lightning sizzled on the horizon.

"Where is the key? Reopen that school! Today!"

"Yes, your Majesty."

Only then could Travancore's ruler enter the ocean to present two handfuls of precious coins in its turbid waters.

As the story goes, on that day Miss Blanford, the missionary, rose from her knees. Ever since the Brahman opposition had forcibly closed the school, she had wrestled in prayer. Now an inner voice assured her all would be well, despite the short violent storm they had experienced.

An hour later a knock sounded at the gate. Her servant hastened to meet the messenger and returned with a packet and envelope, both bearing the royal seal. Miss Blanford opened the letter to read, "The Maharajah desires the school to continue." The packet held the keys.

"Thank God! Oh, thank God," she exclaimed. "The Lord has done it!"

Thus a story was born that persists among Travancore's long lists of intrigue, plunder, and glory.

The number of girls grew from twenty to sixty. Today enrollment is upwards of seven hundred. Education for girls in Kerala State has become widespread.

Johannen reluctantly moved his family from Kodukulanji to Trivandrum when his youngest was six. They lived on the Zenana Mission Compound. Big Aleyamma resumed her teaching in the Fort School for Girls, and enrolled both daughters while John entered a school for boys.

Johannen, now bereft of family, returned home to a house full of memories. He soon sold the property to a near relative while he spent his days in evangelistic work with Mr. Pete.

Little Aleyamma found city life confining, but she became an apt pupil and took the Maharajah's annual award for her class as outstanding pupil until the family again moved from Trivandrum.

When Aleyamma was eleven, due to a new policy that forbad couples being given separate church assignments, thus forcing them to work and live apart, Johannen and Aleyamma moved to Kunnam village in central Travancore. There Johannen served as pastor-teacher. A school for girls had also opened in this town, so Annamma and her younger sister, Aleyamma, enrolled. The Anglican Bishop, highly pleased, commended Johannen publicly for taking the step of leaving Trivandrum.

# Early marriage

On a hot afternoon, about two years later, Johannen looked up from reading a letter to hear his wife say, "We must raise a dowry for Aleyamma."

"What? What did you say?"

"We must find a dowry for Aleyamma."

"But she's a mere child!"

"Hmmm . . . you haven't noticed? She's thirteen, and maturing early. With her exceptional beauty and strong will, Johannen, take my word for it, we're in for some problems! We've got to get her married."

"Our baby?"

His wife turned to pounding spices by pestle and mortar. No other sound broke the silence except a deep sigh from the grey-haired man who said at last, "You're right, my dear. This is the last assignment from the church before I retire. That day comes too soon, but when it does, we'll return to the city."

"Well, we'd better face things as they are."

"Which means we'll have to plan a double wedding, so that the dowry we receive for our son will pay for Aleyamma's expenses."

In due time, after the proper routines of arranging marriages were set in motion, beautiful young Aleyamma was marked for K.C. Oommen, an educated young man living in Krishnapuram with his widowed mother. In Travancore, as in all of the subcontinent, marriages were prearranged. Each couple could but hope that heaven would ratify that which had been done on earth and bless the marriage.

Aleyamma's was no exception. K.C. Oommen, however, had young blood flowing through his veins, and to him seeing his intended was more important than all the mundane details of lineage and dowry. He approached his uncle, the middleman. "I'd like to see her," he pleaded. "You say she's beautiful?"

"Exceptionally so, I'd say." Uncle Josh smiled, looking into the face of his lanky nephew. "Sit down, I'll tell you more."

"But please, couldn't we go to her house?"

"No, Oommen, definitely not!"

"But I want to see her. I must . . ." the twenty-year-old insisted. "There must be a way."

"Let me think about it, Oommen," Uncle Josh said, rumpling his hair.

Several days later the two hid in sight of Pastor Johannan's well at the back of the house. Uncle Josh conjectured that Aleyamma might bring clothes to wash about now, and he was right. There she was, swinging down the path, clothes bucket in hand, and a mischievous laugh at the antics of a mother and baby monkey she was watching.

"We'll walk past the well," Uncle Josh whispered. "I'll lead; you follow, and take a good look."

But instead of walking past, young Oommen stopped as the girl set her clothes bucket down. "Please, could you give me a drink?" he inquired.

She looked up, her black eyes dancing merrily. "Of course," she replied while drawing water. He cupped his hands to drink, but the water slid through his fingers while he gazed, enraptured, on the face of his intended. "You are so beautiful," he murmured.

Aleyamma blushed and hid her face, then looking up said with a laugh, "You don't want to drink? Who are you?"

"Oommen of Krishnapuram," he admitted.

"Oh!" Aleyamma turned to flee, but he pleaded, "I really do need a drink. Don't go. . . ."

Perhaps that little preview helped the young couple through the engagement and wedding ceremonies. Aleyamma loved the excitement, the trousseau and all the attention, but she sensed a growing dread about leaving the familiar for the unknown. Oommen, she felt she could handle, but what about his mother?

Not without reason did Aleyamma fear, for life under the new regime became a horrible nightmare for the young bride who soon gave birth to a son. Oommen loved Aleyamma, but felt he must also please his mother who insisted that the girl was a n'er-do-well, not fit for motherhood. Aleyamma wrote, "We're so different in our upbringing. I can't help but rebel, and so he beats me often. Then I beat my breast and dash my head against a wall. But where is God in all this?"

Where indeed? The girl had grown up in an atmosphere of understanding and love, and now she lived under the rod. She returned to her parents, now in Trivandrum, for the birth of her second child. Oommen followed her, and made the choice to leave his mother and live with his wife and family in Trivandrum. He sustained them through medical work, dispensing homeopathic medicines, along with other jobs.

Aleyamma definitely knew much about the Lord Jesus Christ, but as yet she didn't know *him*. Marital troubles kept rising, mainly because of her love for expensive living, both in foods and clothing. This led to constant bickering between husband and wife, and motivated Aleyamma to get a job as sewing mistress in the Fort School for Girls where her brother, John, now served as headmaster. It was a prestigious position, placing her in touch with homes of royal society, but it increased friction between Oommen and herself. She insisted on buying silks and gold orna- ments when their growing family of five children needed sup- port. They struggled financially, moving often.

Throughout her teaching years in the Fort School for Girls, Aleyamma knew true friendship from two co-workers who band- ed together to pray for her conversion. One, Mrs. Joseph, with her husband, convinced Oommen and Aleyamma to join with them in buying a plot of land near the coast, about three miles from the school. A big change occurred in Aleyamma's life in that small cottage by the sea.

## *Discovery*

Aleyamma had just celebrated her thirty-sixth birthday when her eldest son, Unni, left home after a shouting match.

"I tell you, I'm not staying in this house any longer," he cried, pushing his clothes into a tin trunk.

"Stop it, Unni! Don't be foolish! Where are you going?"

"None of your business," he muttered, "but if you want to know, I've bought a taxi and can take care of myself."

"You what?"

Unni faced his mother, pushed his black hair out of his eyes and screamed, "I'm fed up with the bickering and quarreling in this house! If you think we're hooked on your brand of religion, forget it! I don't want to ever hear of God and the church again!"

"Son, please!" She clutched at her chest as though experienc- ing pain.

"No, Mom! I've had enough." He pushed the last clothes in, banged the top shut, locked it, picked it up, and walked out the door while Aleyamma and her eldest daughter, Chinnakutty, watched. Tears coursed down her cheeks, and mother and daugh- ter sobbed silently together.

Her spirit broke that day, leaving her forlorn and searching for God, but Oommen seemed to get colder, more removed. He was cynical, and his criticism hurt. The family didn't dare cross their father, so mother and children took refuge with the family next door, the Josephs, who were true children of God.

One day Aleyamma burst out, "Where is God? No! If there is a God, he would not give me so much suffering!" This followed an intense quarrel in which Oommen shouted that his wife's love for food caused disruption, in return for which she refused to eat for three days. Now Achamma Joseph, her friend, tried to reason with her.

"You're not alone in your suffering, Aleyamma," she said. "Trouble is universal. Your condition is multiplied over and over again, because people are foolish . . . like sheep! You know how sheep act, don't you?"

No response.

Achamma continued, "You've seen sheep . . . running here and there on their own inclination, doing what they think best. Well, my dear, you've done that for thirty-six years. Isn't it time to let the Good Shepherd take over?"

"What do you mean? I read and pray! You know I do! I send the children to Sunday school."

"Quite, quite different," her friend said softly. "Come with me on Sunday to the nice little Salvation Army mission down by the ocean. You like Captain Elias, I know."

Captain Elias ministered to the poor fisherfolk, but Aleyamma would never allow her children to attend the services because of differences in social status. They must remember they were Syrian Christians. The mission was out-of-bounds.

But one Sunday morning, after another quarrel at home, Aleyamma gathered her family together and left her husband sitting morosely on the bed. They joined the Josephs, saying, "We're coming with you to the mission today."

That service proved the turning point in Aleyamma's life. She says in her journal, "I didn't hear the text. All I heard was that our trouble results from not experiencing the resurrection life of our Lord Jesus Christ. He died and rose for the remission of our sins!

"This pierced my heart like a knife, and I trembled. I felt as though my chest was bursting. I experienced what is written in the Bible. Jesus still works miracles! My ears were opened, my tongue loosened! I felt a deep conviction for sin, the sin of not knowing or loving my Lord Jesus. I wanted to pray. A power I had never known before pervaded my entire being."

Captain Elias noticed her deep conviction, and said, "Let the doctor's wife pray."

She writes, "I don't know how long I prayed, but after I finished, Achamma held my hand and asked, 'What happened?' I said, 'I got a blessing. Jesus came into my heart.' I started singing, 'Rolled away, every burden of my heart rolled away.' I sang all the way home. Yes, I left that morning as a godless mother—and returned with Jesus!"

Her first witness, other than that which she gave in the humble grass shed near the ocean, was to her husband. She found him still seated on his bed. Bursting in, she said, "I got a spiritual blessing today. Jesus came into my heart!"

He muttered, "Only today? He didn't come before?"

"Come, come, everybody!" she called. "I want to tell you about it."

They unrolled prayer mats, and even the servants joined in to hear her sing and witness to new life in Christ. She said it felt like a cool breeze blowing through her, that her heart was like a thoroughly swept granary.

The first of eighteen visions came to Aleyamma Oommen that night, about one o'clock. She suddenly awoke to a light touch but didn't see anyone. Sitting up, she heard a voice say, "My daughter, get up and pray. I have forgiven your sins. Now you must learn to intercede for multitudes."

From that moment she accepted a ministry of intercession that expanded through the years. Every night, while others slept, Aleyamma prayed.

Several days after her conversion she sensed extreme discomfort after eating food. This continued for six months. She found she could take only fruit and water, a diet that barely maintained her physically. Oommen's wife grew weaker and weaker until she found it impossible to breastfeed the baby, Gracy. She sold her gold earrings and bought a cow to give the baby adequate nourishment. However, in spite of illness, Aleyamma never broke her nightly tryst in prayer.

Her husband grew more and more taciturn. Instead of welcoming his wife's transformation, he thought her mentally unbalanced and constantly opposed her.

## *The call*

One night Aleyamma Oommen received her call to preach. She had awakened as usual at one o'clock to pray and knelt on her prayer mat when the awareness of an intense light startled her. She thought a ship must have anchored off shore with its bright lights shining through her west window. But after looking again, Aleyamma decided the brilliance originated inside the room, not outside. It covered her, and she heard a voice saying, "Daughter, I have blessed you. I am the living God. Proclaim me everywhere."

She fell at her Lord's feet, only to feel great physical pain and extreme thirst. When the vision faded, the pain remained, and she found she couldn't talk. Oommen awoke to ask, "Is something wrong?" After indicating she wanted a drink, he arose and gave her water, but it failed to quench her thirst. Achamma Joseph's earnest prayer next morning stopped the pain, but Aleyamma spent the next three days in bed.

On Sunday morning she suddenly heard a voice saying, "Consider yourself to be dead unto sin and alive unto righteousness." Her family has often wondered whether she suffered something like crucifixion. For over thirty-six years she had lived for herself; now she knew another allegiance. By the power of God she jumped out of bed and began rejoicing in the Lord.

The house servants spread the word that the doctor's wife had gone mad. People flocked in, filling the place, but even as they listened and mocked, Aleyamma continued testifying. Oommen tried all kinds of medication, to no profit. The day dragged on.

That night Aleyamma wept and prayed, still smarting under the pressures and misunderstanding of husband and community. Again, as in a vision, she felt a sharp awl thrust through her toe, and the Lord said, "It hurts, doesn't it? Your husband and children are part of you, members of your body. If they oppose you, bear it, but pray for them."

Aleyamma looked up, drying her tears, and began a special prayer vigil for the family that proved very effective through the years. Even though Oommen opposed her considerably longer, he, too, eventually turned to the Lord and joined his Aleyamma in the great ministry God had ordained for them.

## Public ministry

Changes in the Fort School administration caused Aleyamma's brother to return to Kodukulanji to open a high school that still bears his name. Many teachers left at the same time, since the two missionary ladies retired to be replaced by younger people who followed new policies.

Aleyamma fasted and prayed. She felt God leading her to a wider ministry, but surely he wouldn't bring a cleavage in their family life? Could it be?

How could she leave Oommen with five children to support? Unni was on his own, of course, and John had turned twenty-one. In any case, Oommen could support the two boys from his medical earnings, but the girls?

The Lord spoke, telling her to ask for a year's leave of absence and take the girls with her. Down on her face on the prayer mat, Aleyamma awaited further instructions. How could she live, and where?

An Indian couple came to mind. She knew the Alexanders were godly people who supported an orphanage along with maintaining a daily round of visitation and night meetings in a hall near their quarters in Trivandrum.

Her obedience brought a great change to the Oommen family. Chinnakutty's education stopped for lack of funds to pay fees. Lilly remained in school, and Gracy was preschool. Aleyamma wrote, "We had no income. I moved into Mr. Alexander's orphanage with my three girls and aided in their open air meetings and house-to-house visitation. But the children and I were on the brink of poverty. Their education was in shambles, and I became the butt of everyone's ridicule."

In Aleyamma's extremity, the Lord once more encouraged her. He had called her to proclaim him; she must learn to walk by faith. Now she regimented her intercession ministry, eating only one meal a day, and fasting and praying every Tuesday and Friday. The Lord encouraged her many times. In her eighth vision the Lord stood by her, saying, "Don't fear, daughter. I am with you."

Despite this comfort, the girls often went to bed hungry because Aleyamma insisted on having their own kitchen arrangements to preserve some sort of family cohesion. She sold her last gold ornament during that year, as well as household items, to buy food. But she never questioned God.

It was a purifying process. Aleyamma Oommen had loved luxurious living all her life. Now the Lord removed all that, along with her ornaments and expensive clothes. She experienced the purifying of fleshly desires as she grew in her intimacy with God.

This gave way to a spiritual ministry of great power.

# The gospel team

The wind of the Spirit had begun to blow in Trivandrum in those days, and across the land the Lord's people were beginning to sense a new motivation for witness to non-Christians. One day three young men came to Trivandrum from evangelist Kochu Kunju of Marthandam. At his suggestion they joined Aleyamma to form a gospel team. This was amazing, for previously the evangelist had strongly opposed the ordination of women, or their extensive use in a spiritual ministry. Kochu Kunju stated flatly that a woman's place is in her home!

Then he met Aleyamma. Somehow he became convinced of her unique call, and did all he could to aid!

As a side arm of his evangelistic outreach, he had also established an orphanage. Four girls from there soon joined the newly formed gospel team that also included Aleyamma's second son, John. His hefty physique proved a decided asset. In fact, John became his mother's strong arm in place of Unni, her eldest. Lilly's sweet singing voice placed her in the team, but Chinnakutty remained at home, bearing the responsibility of caring for the family.

The gospel team began to move to nearby cities, areas with large Hindu populations. Alleppey, Cherthala, and Aimanan all saw week-long crusades. Often they extended to two weeks. With the anointed preaching of the young men and Aleyamma's fiery witness, these crusades attracted thousands of people.

Her year away from the schoolroom passed before she realized. Too soon she returned to face the new principal. She wrote: "A great door has opened to me. In each meeting we've ministered to crowds of people, but now my year has finished. I suppose I should have expected it, but yesterday I asked Miss Taylor for another year's leave. She has refused. She said flatly, 'Aleyamma, your duty is to care for your children and husband . . . and do the schoolwork. It's not your business to preach.'

"But I've seen the power of God working! I've seen the transformation of those who trust God for forgiveness and cleansing! And I've heard God's voice telling me to proclaim him to everyone. How can I do less? So I answered, 'Please, Miss Taylor, the same God who brought you to India from England has called me to preach the gospel. I would like another year's leave.'

"'Never mention it again,' the English lady said flatly. 'Either you work here, or you have the privilege of resigning.' It came as a shock, but I have resigned. Today, on June 27, 1932, in Miss Taylor's bungalow, I've ended it all. Then I asked for their prayer support, and to my amazement she said, 'Your prayer will be sufficient.' So I prayed aloud, 'Lord, I don't deserve to be employed in this school. You gave me this job out of your bounty. Now I surrender it at your feet. Thank you, Lord. Amen.'"

From the lips of witnesses many claim that from that day Aleyamma Oommen became God's voice for revival, a flash of fire on a decadent, ritualistic society. Her power stemmed from her complete surrender to Jesus Christ. Her ministry of intercession undergirded her public meetings, and miracles followed.

People describe her as being tall, beautiful, with olive-skinned complexion, wavy black hair parted in the middle. Always clad in white, always smiling, she enthralled her listeners with a wealth of lyrics, devotional music that poured out in worship to God. People came to ridicule and heckle, but stayed to pray. In every village and marketplace the Holy Spirit convicted sinners and saved multitudes. Their public testimonies electrified her hearers, and villagers followed Aleyamma Oommen and the team from one crusade to the next.

Her message startled them. She constantly emphasized the need for a personal relationship with Jesus Christ, leading to a transformed and holy life. Given in the transparency that emanated from her own selfless commitment to the Lord, her challenge to walk with God pierced every heart.

Aleyamma desired God himself, rather than his blessings. She never sought proofs or supernatural experiences, yet the Lord gave her eighteen visions to strengthen and guide in times of bewilderment.

Her public ministry must be examined in the context of misunderstanding and outright opposition from the religious leaders of her day, much like that suffered by her Lord. Not strange! He promises persecution to those who obey him. But she never doubted God's call, and in return he authenticated it. She even gained the confidence of the Anglican bishop, with whose letters of commendation her crusades moved outside of Travancore. But that came later.

# *Learning to walk by faith*

Two years after Aleyamma's resignation from the Fort School, years in which she suffered financially, evangelist Kochu Kunju moved his orphanage of about two hundred children and adults from Marthandam to Trivandrum. However, he remained in his former location. On his insistence, Aleyamma Oommen took charge of the orphanage and located it in a large building at the rear of her uncle's immense compound in the heart of the city. She named it Saradam.

The new arrangement released her financially, but involved her with Kochu Kunju's team. Indeed, her fiery preaching and Spirit-filled music greatly impacted his meetings, but she had yet to learn that the Lord could sustain her without the aid of others.

Living in community is hazardous at any time, especially where strong wills meet. Aleyamma, always strong-willed, eventually clashed to the point of cleavage.

It happened when she protected a former prostitute and took her into the orphanage. The repentant woman sought and found God's forgiveness, but Aleyamma's sheltering her raised Kochu Kunju's wrath, not his mercy. He rushed to Trivandrum upon receiving a report from several ladies who disapproved of her action. The evangelist interrogated Aleyamma in front of a hastily summoned panel. "Why did you give asylum to such a woman?" he demanded.

"My brother," she asked, "what would you have done had your daughter been in her shoes?"

"Whoever it is," Kunju shouted, "even my daughter, I'd tie her to a banana stalk and float her down the river Pamba!"

"I'll believe that when I see it," Aleyamma replied.

"What? You dare talk to me like this? I've never had a woman confront me before. You're finished! You'll never stand on my platform again. Never!"

Without flinching the tall woman replied, "My brother, the Lord called me, not you. He has given you a thousand to hear his word. He is faithful enough to provide me with ten thousand." She turned and left the room. The two evangelists parted, and Kochu Kunju moved the orphanage and his team members back to Marthandam.

It happened at a particularly awkward time for Aleyamma. She had just applied for a government grant for the orphanage and expected formal inspection momentarily. Now, with the bulk of the children removed and only her immediate family plus a handful of poor adults on the grounds, she cried to the Lord. "What shall I do?" she pleaded.

"Call for your husband."

"Oommen? Will he come?"

"I've been working in his heart. It is my timing."

When Oommen came, Aleyamma rejoiced to learn that God had humbled his proud spirit, and won him. They became a team together, with quarrels a thing of the past. Now they sought to do only that which pleased their mutual Lord. Chinnakutty says of her parents, "I remember my parents as being amiable and loving from this time onward."

However, to hold down expense, they moved Saradam to another location, providing ample space for forty orphans and additional staff. Its spacious compound adapted well to the needs of lively, growing children. Oommen conducted a school, meeting the educational need, and administered the place while Aleyamma and her gospel team continued answering calls for city-wide crusades. Chinnakutty, her eldest, took the responsibility at home while her mother, sister, and two brothers ministered elsewhere.

Chinnakutty reminisces, "All of us children learned to pray from seeing Ammachi (Mother) pray. We prayed for our daily bread, and we learned to trust God's promises. He never failed! We lived with miracles!

"I recall going without food for a whole day while all of us prayed. Just before noon of the second day, a horse-drawn carriage arrived bearing a large consignment of staples. God had answered again.

"Another time, mother returned from a preaching mission to find us without either food or money. She, too, had nothing more to give, nothing but the *thali*—the gold chain she received at her wedding, something like your wedding ring. I saw mother take the chain from her neck and sing,

> *'Jesus has promised me a golden chain,*
> *Not made with the gold of this world,*
> *But with the gold of Zion's streets.'"*

On another occasion Aleyamma Oommen returned from a campaign to find the rice bins empty. The matron came running and said, "Ammachi, we'd starve if you hadn't come now. I've looked for you every day."

"Isn't there any rice or money?" Aleyamma asked.

"Not a coin! Not a grain!"

Aleyamma prayed silently, then sensing direction, said, "Put the large pot of water on to boil, sister, and we'll call the children to prayer."

She told her enlarged family about the meetings, the wonderful answers to prayer with sick people being healed and large numbers saved. That led to earnest prayer. Aleyamma concluded, her arms lifted and tears rolling down her cheeks, "Lord," she said, "please don't let these little ones starve! You've led me wonderfully these past years. I'm ready to bear any hardship for your name's sake. Now please supply the needs of these little ones."

A hush descended over the group, and Aleyamma began to thank God for hearing and answering. Someone started a praise song, during which they heard a knock at the door.

"John, you get it," Aleyamma said, nodding to her hefty son. He opened to four high-caste Hindu ladies. "We've heard about the orphanage and your beautiful music. Please, you were singing right now. Won't you sing some more?"

"Of course," Aleyamma said with a smile.

One of the ladies handed a bundle of currency to her and murmured, "For the children."

The visitors listened to one song after another, then toured the grounds. When they came to the kitchen, one of the ladies lifted the lid of the large vessel. "What are you cooking?" she asked.

"The rice we bought with the money God sent by your hands," Aleyamma responded softly.

Chinnakutty concluded her many memories asking, "Do you wonder we children learned to trust, even when we could not see?"

One of Aleyamma's staff members from Saradam reminisced as Chinnakutty, my husband, and I sat with our host on his verandah in Kodukulanji. P.N. Ninan, a slightly built gentleman now retired from serving as Director of the Civil Aviation Department for the government of India, has served in high places. As he spoke of past experiences, I noticed again the church on the hill and mused that much had transpired since little Aleyamma first worshiped there with her parents and family.

Ninan said, "As a seventeen-year-old boy, I learned that God works in our extremities. I have proven this throughout my lifetime. Earlier, I served with Mrs. Oommen in the orphanage, but later I became a member of the gospel team. I cherish the memory of both periods."

He mentioned an incident in one of the crusades. "Immense crowds followed her in Adoor. She had a magnetic personality. I'd characterize her messages as simple, but filled with the power of the Holy Spirit. Mrs. Oommen was a truly great woman!"

He vividly remembered one evening when the team faced a challenge. Villagers asked them to pray for a demon-possessed young man who frothed at the mouth and was chained because of being violent. "Joseph and George tried first," Ninan said, "but they couldn't do anything. The demons shouted, 'Who are you? We don't know you.'

"Mrs. Oommen took me with her and we approached him. She spoke quietly but firmly, and four demons argued with her for about an hour. Finally they agreed to leave the young man if they could enter the Hindu temple. Mrs. Oommen said, 'All right, we'll take you there.'

"We placed the young man in a car, seated between Mrs. Oommen and myself. When we neared the Hindu temple, he began to shiver and groan. Then he turned to Mrs. Oommen and asked in a perfectly sane voice, 'Who are you?'

"'We're your friends,' she replied, 'and we're taking you home with us.'"

The young man's deliverance impressed the entire neighborhood. He stayed with the team for about two weeks, completely cured.

## Two decades of public ministry

Aleyamma writes in her journal, "We came to Mavelikara and stayed in the Mar Thoma priest's house. I had a vision there. I saw a host of white-clad angels descending from heaven. From the next day onward, God worked in mighty power, but the Jacobites rose up in protest against it."

Simple words, fraught with drama.

How did a Mar Thoma priest happen to extend hospitality to a controversial woman evangelist and her team? Had he, too, experienced personal revival? What led to Aleyamma's vision?

Discouragement? She doesn't say, but the outright opposition resulting from God's manifested power would testify to the effect of the meetings.

In Mallepally several eyewitnesses mentioned a young man's conversion that impacted the entire area. Quarrelsome and rebellious, this rowdy caused trouble in the open air campaign. The team prayed specifically for him and the next night his open confession with tears moved everybody.

In another town, the wooden platform had been constructed by tying planks together with ropes. Some scoundrels cut them at various places and waited for it to fall during the evening service. Unnoticed, a boy had watched their prank! He informed Aleyamma's teammates, and they reinforced the platform to make it more secure than before. The pranksters must have thought the Lord performed a miracle!

In Pallam some would-be persecutors mixed lime and turmeric with water and filled their squirt guns. Then they sought shelter in a tree beside the road where Aleyamma and her team would pass on their way to the crusade site.

As the procession neared, the scoundrels tensed, then squirted colored water on Aleyamma's white garments, also liberally dousing the girls' white clothes. Only when the procession reached the light of the village gas lamps did Aleyamma realize that what she thought was water actually looked like blood.

The hecklers followed the group. They jeered and threatened, but bystanders quickly called the police to thwart any further mischief.

The result? Aleyamma preached under special anointing and power. Her message on Christ's forgiveness of sins through the sacrifice of his own blood on the cross became all the more meaningful because of those blood stains on the preacher's garment. Next evening the miscreants sheepishly approached the platform and publicly asked forgiveness. They said God had dealt with them harshly the night before, leading them to repentance and the sinner's prayer. Their conversion stirred the entire town.

In Kunnamkulam opposition reared its ugly head. Aleyamma's enemies vowed, "If she comes here to preach, we'll stone her and break her legs." Consequently, when she arrived, her friends advised her not to hold public meetings. She spent four days fasting and praying, during which time plague broke out in the town, and many died.

Now Aleyamma knew her course of action. She went quietly to the homes of the bereaved and gave comfort. With her team members she walked unafraid into the affected areas and ministered love to the sick and dying.

The door to the gospel suddenly opened! Many who previously threatened now pleaded with Aleyamma to come to their homes. "Please, Mrs. Oommen," they said, "if you'll just walk through our streets and sing, God will stay the plague because of you."

In a ladies' meeting in Tiruvalla someone brought a sick child, asking Aleyamma to pray for healing. She did, but nothing happened. Why?

The evangelist stopped everything to seek the reason in fasting and prayer, and appalled, recognized hidden pride in her own heart. She repented with hot tears, publicly confessing her sin and acknowledged the chastening of the Lord.

*Aleyamma*

My informant, Mrs. Annamma Chacko, who was there told me that the Spirit of God fell instantly upon the group, moving from one to the next. People confessed hidden sins, found God's forgiveness and cleansing. The power of God spilled over into the town with many seeking God. Now Aleyamma prayed again for the sick child, this time to see her miraculously healed.

Chinnakutty says, "I saw my mother's excellent spirit, her yearning for the highest in the lives of those she touched. Closest to her were her own children. I saw her weep over Unni's rebellion and empathized in her joy at his return. But when I heard that she had advised him to join Kochu Kunju's team so that he could serve under a godly man, I marveled! In her selflessness she gave Unni into the hands of the man with whom she had parted company. She believed in Kochu Kunju's integrity and worth.

"And when Unni desired to come back and join mother's team, she joyfully moved over to induct him as co-evangelist."

She spoke about her father. "He moved the orphanage four times to the areas of mother's crusades. It seems both of them desired this. It provided a semblance of home life, and offered the immediate prayer support by the children, plus giving them visibility in the meetings.

"While located in Adoor, my parents arranged for Unni's marriage with an orphanage girl who served on the gospel team. By this time he served as co-evangelist, yet the community accepted his marriage to an orphan minus either pedigree or dowry!"

Of her own marriage she says, "While the orphanage was located in Kunnamkulam my husband, K.C. Abraham of Cochin, accepted the Lord during mother's crusade in that important port town. He possessed a college degree and business acumen. After his conversion Abraham announced, 'I'm going to marry one of Mrs. Oommen's daughters.' He did, without a dowry!"

## Extended ministry and later years

To this point, our story has been set in Travancore, now called Kerala, but the day came when Aleyamma's burden to evangelize took her to the other side of the high mountains that separated the coastal kingdoms from the British Presidency of Madras. She was as foreign there as though she came from the Middle East.

Topographically, the plains of Madras Presidency, now Tamil Nadu, stretch mile upon mile under a relentless hot sun. With less than half the rainfall of Kerala, its citizens labor over red soil heavy with iron and aluminum content. This makes farming difficult, and erosion occurs far too soon.

Yet the people have carved out cities of note, foremost Madras, with a population of over five million. Many scholars and philosophers, notably Dr. Radhakrishnan, India's second president, have taught in Madras University and walked its halls.

Tradition claims the Apostle Thomas preached in Madras, only to be martyred. His grave site at St. Thomas Mount draws a constant flow of pilgrims.

Christianity, the religion of the British, was considered a foreign import, however, by the Hindu population. It was only for the West, and would remain a passing fad. Hinduism had been ingrained for 4,000 years! Great temples to Shiva are still seen today, along with the erection of groves of "deities" called "guards" of the village. People venerate these gods with an annual animal sacrifice since they are believed to protect the area from harm. This is especially true among tribals living on the Tamil Nadu side of the mountains.

The Lord led Aleyamma and her family to Tamil Nadu, then known as Madras Presidency. They found a friend, Mr. Baker Fenn, who volunteered to care for the orphanage, and after moving the children back to Trivandrum, they ventured farther afield, first to Madras Presidency, and then to Ceylon, now known as Sri Lanka.

Aleyamma's hope that Anglican churches would open for meetings didn't materialize immediately. Instead, she found some reticence on the part of the churches to accept strangers, so she wrote Bishop Moore for a letter of recommendation. Until it arrived, the Oommens confined their meetings to public places or entered homes only on invitation.

But from the very first meeting, Hindus and Muslims came to the Lord. Their open witness shook whole communities, and precipitated both opposition and God's miraculous power evidenced. As a result every church opened to the team!

Aleyamma's journal mentions two godly people, Judge and Mrs. Arumugam, who did much to make the team's acceptance easier during their travels in Madras Presidency. Not only did they care for their physical needs, but helped find contacts in each city.

In Ceylon their ministry gained momentum, stretching over several years. Aleyamma wrote, "I had planned to go on to Singapore, but the Lord hasn't permitted it. With the commendation of the Bishop of Ceylon, we've worked all over the island. We rented a house and stayed there and held crusades in Kandy, Jaffna, and other places. Praise God, he has given us many souls. This time the enemy's attacks have been directed against my health. I've been seriously ill for the past eight months . . . therefore the blank in my journal."

Broken health, caused largely from her many years of fasting and prayer, pursued Aleyamma until the end. She suffered much, finding it difficult to eat.

Returning to India, Aleyamma and Oommen lived for awhile in central Travancore, that had become Kerala, and when health permitted, she served with her son, Unni, as co-evangelist in his crusades.

By this time Chinnakutty and her husband, K.C. Abraham, had moved from Cochin to the new state of Karnataka, and managed a condiments factory on the outskirts of Bangalore. She kept urging her parents to join them, but Aleyamma loved her own country. However, when Chinnakutty had a cataract operation in June 1967, her mother hurried to help her daughter, and stayed, assured that the Lord was leading. She was seventy-two years of age at the time.

Her last years were spent in intercession and Bible reading. With broken health, she wrote, "The Apostle Paul said he was afflicted so he could comfort others in their affliction. I take comfort from this. I am seventy-four now. Thirty-seven years ago, the Lord called me . . . how good is my God! Now I understand how much he loves me."

Chinnakutty says, "Mother's voice weakened physically, but her message became increasingly clear. She knew the end would come soon. She wanted no black on her coffin! Nothing but white! To her, death was a door, the gateway to a glorious life beyond."

Aleyamma left this earth on the morning of June 13, 1974. The next day her body was interred in Hosur Cemetery in Bangalore with the Right Reverend T.S. Joseph, Assistant Bishop of the Central Kerala Diocese, officiating. Large crowds came to the viewing and funeral. Their presence comforted Oommen and his family, and they marveled at the great respect the community paid to this godly woman.

She lived, and died, telling people of the dawn. And in the midst of their tears Oommen and his children knew that for Aleyamma it was no longer night. The dawn had come.

## *About the author*

To Leoda Buckwalter, India is home! Born of missionary parents, she spent much of her childhood in North Bihar, then returned to the United States for high school and college. With her husband, Allen, she served in India for over forty years (1939-1981) and currently resides with her husband in Elizabethtown, Pennsylvania.

The Buckwalters continue serving the cause of missions as Regional Directors of FEBC Radio in the northeastern United States.

Leoda's books include *Silhouette*, *The Chief's Son*, *Window Seat on a Crowded Train*, and *Manorma*, a novel.